ANNIE F. DOWNS

D1568624

LOOKING
FOR
LOVELY

COLLECTING THE MOMENTS
THAT MATTER

GIRLS'
BIBLE STUDY

LifeWay Press®
Nashville, Tennessee

Published by LifeWay Press®

Author is represented by Alive Literary Agency, 7680 Goddard Street, Suite 200, Colorado Springs, CO 80920, *www.aliveliterary.com*.

ISBN 9781430052531• Item 005781390

Dewey decimal classification: 234.2

Subject headings: RELIGION / CHRISTIAN MINISTRY / YOUTH

To order additional copies of this resource, write to LifeWay Church Resources Customer Service; One LifeWay Plaza; Nashville, TN 37234-0113; fax 615.251.5933; phone 800.458.2772; email *orderentry@lifeway.com;* order online at *www.lifeway.com;* or visit the LifeWay Christian Store serving you.

Printed in the United States of America

Cover design: Matt Lehman

Student Ministry Publishing
LifeWay Church Resources • One LifeWay Plaza • Nashville, TN 37234-0144

CONTENTS

ABOUT *the* AUTHOR

ANNIE F. DOWNS is an author, speaker, and blogger based in Nashville, Tennessee. Flawed but funny, she uses her writing to highlight the everyday goodness of a real and present God.

While she loves writing—books, blogs, articles, thank you notes— Annie also enjoys traveling around the world speaking to young women, college students, and adults. Annie is a huge fan of bands with banjos, glitter, her community of friends, boiled peanuts, and football games. Read more at *anniefdowns.com* and follow her on Twitter @anniefdowns.

DEAR FRIEND,

One of my favorite things to do is get coffee with my people. Near my house in Nashville is a coffee shop called Portland Brew. There is a dark side—where there is no natural light and a full brick wall, and there is the light side—full of windows. You can almost always find me sitting on the light side, with an almond milk chai in hand, and a friend across the table from me.

That's where I wrote a lot of this study, and you're the friend I pictured across the way. Sitting around and talking with my friends about the Bible is a real joy for me because I genuinely find the Bible so very interesting. The stories we know, the stories we don't, the humans acting like humans, and the God who loves us like crazy and looks past the sins of our humanness because of Jesus' sacrifice.

I hope you feel that way too. Whether you are going through this study alone (you aren't alone—I'm here too!), or if you are with a group, my prayer is that these few sessions will help you fall more in love with the Word of God and with Jesus, and that you will grow a heart that help you persevere in ways you never have before.

I've been a Christian for a few decades now, but I'm telling you everything changed for me when Romans 5 came to life in my heart and spilled out in my thoughts and actions. I'm praying the same for you. My hope and prayer is that you will see yourself in new ways too. And that you will begin to choose, in new and deeper ways, to rejoice in your sufferings and persevere, so that your character may grow, so that hope is birthed in your life and overflows onto those around you. And that you begin to look for and find the lovely in the midst of it all.

I'm right here with you and I can't wait to study with you.

Sincerely,

Annie

INTRODUCTION

I've always been a quitter. From soccer as a kid to relationships as an adult, when things get difficult, I tend to run away. All of this led to a point in my life I now refer to as "the broken crazy." I decided to change; I *needed* to change. I had to stop quitting. I **needed** to learn to persevere. Once I began the road to not quitting, the road away from "the broken crazy," I realized it was going to take a lot of looking for lovely. I needed to find a reason to show up and not give up. As I thought back over my own life, the beautiful things, though few and far between at times, were the knots on the rope that helped me keep climbing.

There's a correlation, I'm finding, between beauty and perseverance, between looking for lovely and not giving up. And beauty is in the eye of the beholder, isn't it? It's not just in the things that everyone sees, but it's what *you* see, what sticks out to *you*, the unique moments that God gives *you* to collect and hold and draw strength from for the difficult times.

I needed to find lovely if I was going to hang in there. I need it in my life. I need it in my heart. I need it in the bank of my soul to withdraw from when things feel hard. So I decided to start looking.

I've spent significant time over the last few years looking for lovely, actively pursuing it, trying to find it around every corner and ever hoping it's just right there, because I do love beautiful things. But mostly I just don't want to quit anymore. I pulled out old photo albums of trips and memories and I opened my eyes wider (if that's possible, since I already have froggy-wide eyes) to the world around me. In the process, I found Romans 5:3-5. Take a moment to read those verses now. We'll be discussing them in this study and how they show us not to quit.

Romans 5:3-5 teaches us that there are four stages on the path to finding lovely. I've charted them out here.

suffering → perseverance → character → hope

GROUP GUIDE

WELCOME!

If you haven't already, go ahead and read the session introduction on the previous page together as a group.

AS WE BEGIN, DISCUSS THE FOLLOWING QUESTIONS WITH YOUR GROUP:

What do you think it means to "look for lovely"?

What do you hope to gain from this study?

WATCH THE VIDEO:

To hear more from Annie, download the optional teen girls' video bundle to view the Session 1 video at *lifeway.com/girls.*

NOW, LET'S TALK:

How does God remind you of His faithfulness (friends, things you read, nature, etc.)?

Read Romans 5:3-5. What do these verses tell us about perseverance?

When have you struggled not to quit? Did you give up? Why or why not?

How do you think looking for lovely helps us to persevere?

PRAY:

Pray together as a group that you will all learn to look for lovely during the next few sessions. End the time together by praising God for His faithfulness.

DAY 1

BUT FIRST, PEACE

I like to make a smoothie every morning for breakfast. I stumble into the kitchen and pull half a banana and a chopped up peach from The Peach Truck out of the freezer and orange juice, almond milk, and spinach out of the fridge. The goal is to stuff my smoothie with more spinach than I would eat in a salad.

Here's something you should know about me—I don't love salad. I like it fine, but as a girl who has an adult onset allergy to dairy, a salad without ranch and cheese is just sadness. So I don't love eating them. Yet my brain responds really well to green things (yours does too, by the way), and so I try to give it the leaves it wants.

I whir all the ingredients together, add a few chia seeds and some protein powder, and that's my breakfast.

The first time I made a smoothie, I didn't feel all that different. But I did notice as the fruits and vegetables blended together that the colors were beautiful. It was almost mesmerizing to watch. Two years later, my body is healthier, my brain is healthier, my energy level is way up, and my vegetable intake is way, way up.

Something about the white-noise whir of that blender and the colors mixing made it a good morning, over and over again. I needed the beautiful of it, the peace of it, even if it took some time for my body to appreciate the change on the breakfast menu.

Isn't that the truth of perseverance sometimes? Isn't it true in your life also—sometimes it takes seeing the moments of lovely for you to keep going?

What are some ways you look for lovely in your everyday life, like how I love the sight of the colorful fruits mixing in the blender in the morning?

What does the word perseverance *mean to you? Why does perseverance matter?*

*What's one situation you're in right now that requires you
to persevere?*

What's the role of beauty in perseverance? Spoiler alert: It's a big one. If you're going to finish the brave/challenging/hard thing God has called you to do, you have to look for the lovely moments. But you also have to decide persevering and finishing are worth it.

That's it. That's kind of the "thing" here. It's the jar that holds the lovely—your belief that persevering matters. That if you finish—versus quit—you'll be glad you did.

> Let perseverance finish its work so that you may be
> mature and complete, not lacking anything.
> JAMES 1:4

What's the benefit of letting perseverance "finish its work" in your life?

Jot down that verse on a notecard or in your journal. We're going to come back to it again this session, and I want you to have it in front of you as a good reminder of why we persevere. This study, this topic, it's in the center of my heart—it's where I'm living right now, and it's what I've seen God do in my life recently. It has changed me.

READ ROMANS 5:1-5.

*What's the first thing Paul says we have after faith? Why is
that important?*

Without peace, we cannot persevere. We will run out of energy, stamina, and an ability to look around us for the beautiful.

A lot of people look for beautiful things in the world; they try to see lovely when they look around. And I think that's great. But this is different. This is deeper. We are looking for lovely because we are looking for God. We want to see where He is moving, what He has created, and take in that beauty, treating it like the gift from Him that it is.

But before that, we must have peace. And this peace, the one particularly mentioned here in verse 1, is the peace that comes from salvation through Jesus Christ. It's like the baseline peace we can carry with us at all times—because of Jesus, we have peace with God, and we can have peace in God, too.

This peace means two different things to me.

Peace *with* God is a gift given to us when we accept Jesus as our Savior and Lord. He died so that we may be made righteous before God. We can be with God because we are forgiven. That is peace with God.

Peace *in* God is a choice we make again and again—something we can choose to grab onto and wrap ourselves in. We need them both. Peace with God gives us permission to ask and to pursue peace in God. You probably know what peace feels like.

Last summer, some friends and I loaded up picnic baskets and hopped into my friend Matt's antique truck and drove down to Leiper's Fork, Tennessee. It's a little country town that doesn't mind when you visit. We drove out into a field and unpacked our dinner—meats, cheeses, watermelon, chocolate chip cookies, and a pasta salad. We passed around and each stabbed our preferred pieces with our forks. We sat there for hours, talking some of the time but also spending time sitting in silence. As the sun set, I leaned back and watched the sky turn July navy and listened as my friends talked. Right there I felt peace. I felt the feeling of no matter what was going on in my life, in my home, in my work, right here in the back of this pickup truck, all was well. God was near. I recognized it in the way you recognize the smell of your grandmother's house.

Dinner that night didn't change any of the tumultuous situations I was living in, but it was a peace-filled experience I collected in my heart, and it gave me the strength and emotional energy to drive back to town and re-enter my real life. The peace stayed with me once I found it, spilling over into the next day.

What would it look like for you to have peace in your life every day?

For me, finding peace in God feels like stopping. It's quiet. It's listening. It's asking God to calm the waves that are crashing in every corner of me. I take a few long, deep breaths, and I ask Him to be my peace. It's a daily thing for me.

Peace matters. We have to stop and camp there today. I don't know what you need to do, whether it's just pause and breathe for a minute with your eyes closed or have a full out lay-on-your-face moment with God. But I know that the need for peace is real.

> Peace I leave with you; my peace I give you. I do not give to you as the world gives. Do not let your hearts be troubled and do not be afraid.
> JOHN 14:27

Jesus left peace for us. And according to this verse, peace fights against two things.

What are the two things?
1.
2.

Throughout this study, you're going to need to come back here, to a place of peace. It's not about your outside circumstances, though maybe you do need a picnic at sunset. It's actually about your heart. It's about being in a trusting position, a restful position, even when your world seems to be spinning. We will get to everything else—the beauty, the perseverance, the road to the hope that is an anchor—but first, peace.

Journal a prayer asking God to be your peace, to bring you peace, and thank Him that, as it says in Romans 5, we can have peace with God through Jesus Christ.

DAY 2
REJOICE

Let's start where we left off: *peace*. Ask God to be your peace today and to give your mind peace as you study.

I get lost a lot. My friends know that about me. Pretty much everybody knows that about me. Give me verbal directions and you might as well be speaking a different language. I'm just not going to get where you want me to go. I'm really sorry.

Write the directions down? Now we're on the right track. Now we're getting somewhere. (Now I can't come up with a sentence that isn't a bit travel punny.)

As a result, I'm always thinking about how to give directions. I notice lots of landmarks and restaurants, so that when you want me to tell you how to get somewhere, I can give you far more information than you actually want. Because I think you can't overshare when it comes to helping someone get where they want to go.

That's us this session. We are on a road to hope, a path to find the lovely, a journey to believe that the marathon of life is always worth it. And I'm probably giving you way more directions than you want. But it's because I believe in the destination, and even more than that, I believe in the opportunity to get there. The twists and turns and dips in the road are just as important as the finish line.

Let's flip back to Romans 5, where we left off yesterday.

> READ ROMANS 5:1-5.

> *Verse 2 says we rejoice or boast in something. What?*

> *Look in Romans 4 for the faith of Abraham. How did Abraham rejoice in hope? Why does hope matter?*

> *(We're going to come back to hope later. But the path to hope is a little different than we may realize.)*

ROMANS 5:3 mentions a totally different reason to rejoice. Fill in the blank:

"Not only so, but we also rejoice in our _____ ..." (ESV).

I'm not great at rejoicing in my sufferings. I'm not great at looking at a hard or painful situation, whether it was in my control or not, and being grateful for the pain. I don't like pain. I actually tend to run from it.

I'm a quitter. It's a bit in my nature that when things get hard or confusing or smell anything like suffering, I want out. Whether it's a relationship that has tension or a season of hurt or just a hard time that I want to quit or check out of, it often feels easier to do that than to rejoice or glory in my sufferings.

List a few of the ways you are suffering now.

Let's discuss the word used to describe how we are supposed to handle the sufferings we face. It isn't *rejoice,* like throw a party about it and just smile your way through. Both here in verse 3 and back in verse 2 where we're told to rejoice in hope, it uses the same original Greek word. Looking at the definition of the transliteration below, underline the part(s) that stand out to you.

> *kauchaomai* (verb) — to glory, boast, or rejoice;[1] properly, living with "head up high," i.e. *boasting* from a particular *vantage point* by having the *right base of operation* to deal *successfully* with a matter; likely comes from the root, *auxēn* ("neck"), i.e. what holds the head up high (upright); figuratively, it refers to living with *God-given confidence.*[2]

Every situation looks different based on your viewpoint. A finish line looks tiny until you're standing on it. A dress looks different in your own mirror than it does when you're seeing it under dressing room lights. Your view matters.

The thief comes only to steal and kill and destroy; I have
come that they may have life, and have it to the full.
JOHN 10:10

Take a minute and remember that you have an Enemy and he is always creeping around trying to distort your view, trying to have you see your hurts and pains and sufferings through a lens of disappointment and frustration with God. He is always (Do you hear me? *Always.*) trying to steal, kill, and destroy your view.

The last thing he wants you to do on this journey is lift your head and look ahead. He wants you looking at your feet, weighed down and discouraged, lost and alone. Whether any of that is true or not, he wants you to feel it.

That's different from what God tells us to do. What the Bible is saying here is that we are to hold our heads up high in suffering. Not that we aren't allowed to feel or hurt, but that through it, we stand tall.

I was at a campground looking for a little escape for my mind and a little exercise for my body. I asked one of the counselors to suggest a good walk. He pointed me to the road. "There's a major hill, and when you think you've reached the top, it curves left and the hill actually keeps going."

Sounds miserable, I thought. "Sounds great!" I said.

I headed out on the walk and sure enough, the curving hill was legit and I was struggling. I was looking at my feet, resting my hands on my knees as I tried to push myself up the hill. My back was killing me and my thighs were throbbing in that way that isn't like "we're getting stronger" but more like "we're breaking." I stopped for a minute, stood up straight, and stretched. I looked around, maybe for the first time in the thirty minutes I had been on the road.

The green in the trees was incredible. The flowers were just starting to bloom and right there, on the edge of the road, were petals in every shade of pink. I looked up the hill and all the way there were patches of flowers.

I decided to finish the hill differently. I didn't quit. I didn't run from the suffering back down the hill to camp. I just stood up as I continued to walk. It might not have been as fast and determined, but the view was way better. I stood tall, back straight, and I looked straight ahead as I memorized the flowers and took notice of the variety of greens, because colors blow my mind. (Like seriously. The amount of greens in the woods in unreal to me.)

Every bit of the pain changed when my view changed. It didn't go away; it just wasn't my focus anymore. Instead of focusing on my suffering, I began to focus on the beautiful things God had put in my path.

READ EPHESIANS 6:10-19.

Verses 13-14 say that after you have done everything to prepare, what do you do next?

Right. You "stand firm" (v. 14). I picture this as the same type of head-held-high posture, the one that can see the flowers and see the greens even when the hill is still only halfway climbed. But I also can picture someone like my friend, Bianca.

When Bianca walks into a room, she carries herself with confidence, not because she thinks she's the bees knees (spoiler alert: she is), but because she knows God made her on purpose. As a result, no matter what life throws her—and it has thrown her some curve balls—she's sure-footed on the gospel. You can hear it in Bianca's conversations; even if it's through tears, you can hear that she doesn't give up on God. She sees things differently than I do, I think, because of this. She's quick to see the good in the situation because her head doesn't hang down and stare at the dirt (not literally, but also literally). Bianca is an example to me of what it means, even in suffering, to continue to stand.

What loveliness might you see if you stand up tall and confident in God?

There's another reason we glory in our sufferings—because of what it produces.

READ ROMANS 5:3-5 AGAIN.

You're probably not going to like me saying this, but I have to tell you the truth. Suffering matters. Suffering has a purpose. Whether it's suffering in relationships, in health, in your school, or in your spiritual walk, it all has a purpose. It's all shaping who you are and who you become. You need to hold your head high and look around when you're feeling weighed down—because what comes next is so worth it.

Perseverance. Character. Hope. And a way better view.

1. "*kauchaomai,*" Blue Letter Bible, Strong's 2744. Available online at *blueletterbible.org.*
2. "*kauxáomai,*" Helps Word Studies, copyright © 1987, 2011 by Helps Ministries, Inc. Available online from Bible Hub at *biblehub.com.*

DAY 3
DO NOT QUIT

I believe in perseverance. Don't hear me wrong, it's not because I am good at it. I just believe in it because I see it working in my life.

I went to Ecuador in January with Compassion International. I loved every minute of the trip except for the part where all my high school Spanish—from, you know, twenty years ago—was gone from my mind. Words I *know* I used to know could not be recalled and phrases I was supposed to understand quickly took time as I dissected them in my brain.

When I arrived home, I immediately downloaded an app that helps you learn other languages for free. Spanish was going to return to my life, and the front of my mind, so as I wrote letters to my sponsor kids and they wrote me back, it would all make sense. And, if I'm ever lucky enough to return to Ecuador, I wanted to be ready to communicate. (Also, I will bring altitude medicine because good gravy that country is high in the sky.) I was committed to that app for a month. I practiced every night before going to bed. And then, in typical Annie fashion, I quit. I don't know the day I quit. I don't know exactly what knocked me off the learning Spanish wagon, but I fell off and I fell off hard.

I wish I would not have quit. Months later, I would be way closer to speaking the language and I wouldn't feel the guilt and shame I feel right now telling you the story. (I'm going to pick back up with the app tonight, I promise.) Quitting very rarely pans out for me—it always seems to be the easy way out that costs me more in the long run.

I'm no lawyer, and I'm certainly no expert on it, but I want to build a case for you this session, a case for not quitting. You know you need peace. You saw yesterday the posture we're to take in our sufferings—like Abraham, believing beyond hope, standing tall in our hearts, standing on the truth of the gospel, and not giving up.

> *How different would your life be if you made a commitment to persevere—to not quit?*

> *From Romans 5:3-5, fill out these blanks...*

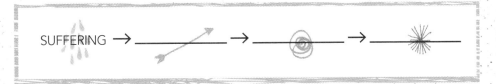

SUFFERING → _____ → _____ → _____

Suffering produces perseverance, and perseverance produces character, and there, after your character is built? Hope.

There isn't enough space or a font big enough to tell you how much I think of perseverance and all the reasons we have to make it a solid pillar of our life. The longer I live this life of faith in Christ, the more I realize perseverance—choosing it, living in it, trusting what it does in your life—is a game-changer.

Next to kindness, courage, and generosity—add perseverance.

> [2] Consider it pure joy, my brothers and sisters, whenever you face trials of many kinds, [3] because you know that the testing of your faith produces perseverance. [4] Let perseverance finish its work so that you may be mature and complete, not lacking anything.
> JAMES 1:2-4

According to James, what's the first thing we are to consider joy?

Trials. Gross. Not fun. Blech. Why does the Bible always seem to start with "get pumped about the hard stuff"? It's the pits, huh? Not exactly a fun truth to deal with.

According to verse 3, what does the testing of your faith develop?

READ JAMES 1:4 AGAIN.

What do you gain when perseverance finishes its work?
1.
2.

Do you think your view of lacking nothing and God's view of you lacking nothing are the same? Explain.

Describe a time when your faith was tested, and after it was over you knew your relationship with God was deeper—when you knew you were more mature as a result of the testing.

And it's this perseverance that produces character in you. Character. Proven. Tried. The human that you are and that you become every day. The part of you that you hope kicks in when decisions need to be made.

It's important to draw a distinction between character and personality. Your personality is who you are, for sure—it's a combination of your likes and dislikes and strengths and weaknesses and experiences. It's the *you* the world sees. Where you are on the introvert/extrovert scale is a great example of your personality.

Your character, on the other hand, is deeper than that—it's the part of you that makes the decision. Your personality is the part that decides how to act out the decision. It's your character that can grow or shrink, be full of light or dark, strengthen or weaken— whereas your personality just displays what has happened in your character.

The word *character* is only used seven times in the Bible, in six passages—all in the New Testament. In the original Greek, *character* is translated *dokimē*.

> *dokimē* (noun) — experience; tried character; proof;[1]
> (1) in an active sense, a proving, trial: through affliction (see 2 Cor. 8:2)
> (2) approvedness, tried character (see Rom. 5:4; 2 Cor. 2:9; Phil. 2:22); exhibited in the contribution (see 2 Cor. 9:13)[2]

Let's look at the passages mentioning *dokimē* and see what it means to let perseverance grow character in us. Look up the following verses and fill in the blanks. (I used the NIV, so that will make your life easier as far as getting the exact words.)

ROMANS 5:4
"... perseverance, _____; and _____, hope."

2 CORINTHIANS 2:9
"Another reason I wrote you was to see if you would _____ _____ _____ and be obedient in everything."

2 CORINTHIANS 8:2

"In the midst of a very severe _____, their overflowing joy
and their extreme poverty welled up in rich generosity."

2 CORINTHIANS 9:13

"Because of the service by which you have _____ yourselves,
others will praise God for the obedience that accompanies your
confession of the gospel of Christ, and for your generosity in sharing
with them and with everyone else."

2 CORINTHIANS 13:3

"... since you are demanding _____ that Christ is speaking through
me. He is not weak in dealing with you, but is powerful among you."

PHILIPPIANS 2:22

"But you know that Timothy has _____ himself, because as a
son with his father he has served with me in the work of the gospel."

What are your observations after looking at the uses of the word and
at the original Greek for "character" in Romans 5? How else is it used?

Why do you think versions of the word "prove" are used repeatedly?
How does our suffering prove who we really are?

It's why we can't quit. Because it proves something every time we hold on. It shows the
world something beautiful—they see it in you, in your character, in the kind of person
you are.

And then? When your sufferings have produced perseverance and that has produced
character? You're on the road to hope.

1. "dokimē," Blue Letter Bible, Strong's 1382. Available online at blueletterbible.org.
2. "dokimos," Thayer's Greek Lexicon, Strong's NT 1382. Copyright © 2002, 2003, 2006, 2011 by Biblesoft, Inc. Available from
   Bible Hub online at biblehub.com.

DAY 4
ALL FOR HOPE

I think we all want to have hope. I mean, we hang the word in our homes and write it in permanent ink on our skin. We tell other people to have it, we want it, but what you and I have both learned in the last few days is that hope isn't a cheap word.

What builds hope according to Romans 5:3-5?

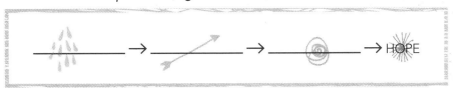

So, hope is the prize. Hope is the end goal. Hope is what grows when the garden of grief and suffering is tended.

That changes the meaning of the word *hope* to me. That takes hope from this average word that people say all the time to a thing I want to treasure in my heart—something that when I feel it, I want to notice it. Because hope means that I survived, I persevered, and my character is stronger because of it.

> We have this hope as an anchor for the soul, firm and secure.
> HEBREWS 6:19a

What is hope according to this verse?

Describe what an anchor does.

This word *anchor* (*agkyra*) is only used in the Bible in one other story.

READ ACTS 27:27-42.

In my NIV Bible, this section of Scripture is labeled "Paul's Shipwreck."

What words come to mind when you think of a shipwreck?

The word anchor *(or anchors) is used three times in Acts 27.
Which verses?*
1.
2.
3.

What this story and these three mentions show us is that an anchor is needed when the storms seem too rough and when the ship needs to stay in place. I like this story (in a I-never-want-to-be-in-that-situation kind of way), because I like how much detail we receive from the author, Luke. I like how strategically the anchors are dropped. And I like how Paul reassured them that they would all be safe. Without the anchors, I'm not sure that would have been true.

The actual definition of *anchor*, from *Merriam-Webster*, is "a heavy device that is attached to a boat or ship by a rope or chain and that is thrown into the water to hold the boat or ship in place."[1]

When does a boat use its anchor?

So, if hope is an anchor, it's what we use in our lives to stay put, to be secured, even when the waters of life are rolling around us. One thing we have to remember is to place our hope in the right things. We drop metaphorical anchors all the time, right? But only when we drop our anchors, or place our hope, in God and His promises, are we truly secure when life gets crazy.

How have you seen that to be true in your life? Where in your life do you need an anchor right now?

READ 1 CORINTHIANS 13:13.

What three things remain?

If hope remains, what other three building blocks of hope must remain as well (this fill-in-the-blank should help…)?

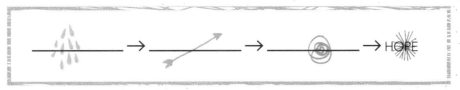

Hope is all over the Bible. It's a theme for David all through the Psalms to Paul's writings in the New Testament. Pull out your Bible and flip to the concordance or use *myWSB.com* or other online Bible sources to search the word "hope."

How do these verses with "hope" referenced in them remind you of hope as an anchor for your life? How do these verses apply to your life or current situation?

Back to our original question: What's the role of beauty in perseverance? If we live Romans 5, then we have hearts that rejoice, even on the tough days. And as we rejoice, we learn to keep going, to fight against the urge to give up when it feels too hard. And that builds something in us—an ability to hold our heads high as we're persevering. It grows our character. And then as we stand tall, our eyes are looking outward, able to see the lovely things, able to hope.

List three lovely things about your week so far.

1.

2.

3.

In what areas of your life do you need hope? Journal a prayer below asking God to give you eyes to see light and joy around you.

---

1. anchor, *Merriam-Webster*, 2016. Available online at *http://www.merriam-webster.com/dictionary/anchor.*

Session 2

FARMERS

We call it Georgia red clay. It's not like normal dirt. It's thick and breaks off in chunks and is, well, red. Totally red. It doesn't dust up around you when you run; it packs down beneath you. It stains your shoes and shorts. And it's as much a part of my southern-bred childhood as boiled peanuts and lightning bugs.

I wasn't raised by farmers; I was raised by lawyers. So I'm not going to sit here and pretend to understand the life and times of a farm family. The best I can tell you is that we had grapevines, red clay, and a gravel driveway, and my grandparents both had a far more farm-like life than I ever did. My grandmother would tell us stories while we picked the muscadine grapes about life as a cotton farmer. Yet it wasn't until I went off to college at the University of Georgia out of my metro-Atlanta circle and made friends with some South Georgia folk that my farming education really began.

A bunch of us went home with Ashley for a weekend, and in true college fashion, we showed up caravan style after our four-hour drive and piled on beds to take naps.

That night at dinner, we sat down to enjoy homegrown food, and as Ashley's dad prayed to bless the food, he prayed for the soil and the rain. I had never heard anything like that before it was later explained to us that the soil needed to be just right and the rain needed to come for the crops to grow so their family would have produce to sell.

We later went out to see the pecan trees, the fields, and the family's livelihood. It was fascinatingly beautiful and educational.

Farming is a central career featured all throughout the Bible, from Adam and Eve being instructed to take care of the land to Jesus often using agricultural metaphors in His teachings. I don't know another job choice that better understands the planting, the waiting, the toiling, the trusting, and the harvest—the hope—than farmers. Farmers, perhaps more than any of us, understand how to look for lovely in the midst of waiting, to find purpose in the days between planting and harvesting, to see God in the middle.

GROUP GUIDE

WELCOME!

Before you begin discussing this session's personal study, talk as a group about what you've found during this study as you've looked for lovely. What lovely things have crossed your path? If you haven't already, go ahead and read the session introduction on the previous page together as a group.

AS WE BEGIN, DISCUSS THE FOLLOWING QUESTIONS WITH YOUR GROUP:

How does peace in God affect our everyday lives?

Do you know someone like Bianca, who holds their head high? What does that say about them?

How have you seen hope as an anchor for your life?

WATCH THE VIDEO:

To hear more from Annie, download the optional teen girls' video bundle to view Session 2 at *lifeway.com/girls*.

NOW, LET'S TALK:

Read Hebrews 12:1-2. How do you fix your eyes on Jesus?

What changes in your life when you focus on Christ?

What, if any, experience do you have with farming? Share your experiences with the group.

PRAY:

Pray together, thanking God for hope. Ask Him to help you to learn to persevere through sufferings. Pray for specific trials that girls in your group are walking through.

DAY 1

THE PARABLE OF THE SOWER

Before we dive into the life of a farmer, consider what you do know about farming. And I'm not just talking about songs like "Farmer in the Dell" and "Old MacDonald." (To be fair, I still enjoy them at the appropriate time.)

What do you think we can learn from gardeners and farmers—the ones who work the land—about pursuing life?

I'll never forget my friend Ashley's dad praying specifically for the soil when we visited them in college. It stuck out to me. As a tomboy kind of gal who always had her hands or feet in the dirt, I just remember thinking how I had played in it all my life but never thought to pray for it. My life didn't depend on it, my well-being didn't rely on it. Yet for the sower, the soil is everything.

Matthew 13 starts with a parable, a story that Jesus tells, all about soil and seeds.

READ MATTHEW 13:1-9.

Match the four types of soil to the result after being scattered by the farmer.

Fell on the path	*Scorched by the sun*
Fell on rocky places	*Produced a crop*
Fell among thorns	*Birds ate it up*
Fell on good soil	*Grew up but choked*

Farmers and gardeners and all those who work with soil have to be intentional and watchful when they are planting seed. And patient. Patient for days. You may not be planning to go out and toss seeds across the yard today, but there's a lot we can learn from this story when it comes to making the choice to persevere and *enjoy* the process of sowing seeds intentionally and wisely.

First of all, Jesus actually explained exactly what this parable is about. (I appreciate when He did that.)

READ MATTHEW 13:18-23.

Jesus explained that the seed represents the Word of God. And He clarified what each of the four soils from the story represent. Record them below.

Fell on the path = _____

Fell on rocky places = _____

Fell among thorns = _____

Fell on good soil = _____

Why do you think Jesus took time to explain this parable to His disciples?

Why was it important for them to know that this story was about how people will receive the message of the gospel?

This parable is also written in two other Gospels. I often think that if multiple guys took time to write down a story, it's worth us taking note. There's something God wants us to understand.

READ MARK 4:1-20 AND LUKE 8:1-15.

Copy Luke 8:15 here.

By enduring, by persevering, Jesus says seed on good soil will produce a crop.

Thinking back to last session, what's a good fruit you know that perseverance produces (look back at Rom. 5:4)?

This soil and seed story reminds me of how we handle hard times. Go with me here. When I consider these seeds and their challenges, and the challenges I'm facing right now in my life (that have nothing to do with actual dirt and seed), I think about a couple of different ways I can approach the hard moments.

I'm about to do my first workout with a new trainer. Nothing happens after a first workout except soreness. Like majorly sore—even my feelings are hurting kind of sore. And I'm guessing I'll want to quit after today. I'm tempted to be like the second kind of soil in this story. I'm tempted to give up in the face of my trials. I have the choice, right now, to decide what kind of soil I'm going to be when this gift of gaining strength is dropped on me. However, I know if I endure and persevere and let this seed grow, I'm going to be stronger and healthier.

The same is true for any challenge that comes our way. We have to be receptive soil to God's Word, His promises, and who He is. When we plant seeds of Scripture and the loveliness of the character of God continually in our hearts, when we are good soil, receptive to those seeds, we will be able to persevere. We will produce fruit.

Even before I start today, I have to get my mind right. I have to prepare to be receptive soil.

If you're the soil, what does it look like to be prepared for God to grow something in you?

How do we continually plant the seeds of God's Word in our lives?

What will it look like, in a few months, when the seed God has planted in your good soil has grown? What will that look like for a crop to be produced?

Farmers and gardeners know a little something about getting the soil right—they add to it, they turn it over, they prepare it for the seed. Our prayers today should be that God will make us good soil, ready for the seed that will produce a crop.

DAY 2

THE PARABLE OF THE MUSTARD SEED

I love how Jesus just kept on with the farming parables in Matthew 13.

What does that tell you about the crowd who gathered to hear Him teach?

What did Jesus have to do to be able to teach such a large crowd (v. 2)?

These folks get water life and farming life (both which require significantly more perseverance than, say, my Instagram life). So Jesus, taking eternal lessons and putting them in everyday language, made gospel truth available for the people standing right in front of Him. I love that. He didn't water down the truth, but He framed it in a way that helped the people understand.

I've been staring at pictures of mustard seeds and mustard plants all day. I'm a color fanatic—bright colors in large groups (like fireworks) are my favorite. So to see my Google browser just covered in mustard yellow is a gorgeous thing.

In my life as a Bible-reading Christian, I've heard one "mustard seed" story told over and over again.

> He replied, "Because you have so little faith. Truly I tell you, if you have faith as small as a mustard seed, you can say to this mountain, 'Move from here to there,' and it will move. Nothing will be impossible for you."
> MATTHEW 17:20-21

What does Jesus say about faith and a mustard seed?

That has always been the correlation for me. Mustard seed faith = moving mountains. I've never seen it done, but I've pictured it in my mind a thousand times. But come to find out, that's not even His most famous mustard seed story. The one in Matthew 13 is also told by Mark and Luke (like the parable of the sower), and I feel like this may be the first time I've ever noticed this story. (I should put some sort of "I must have missed it because the parable is as small as a mustard seed" joke here, but I won't do that to you. I respect you more than that.)

READ MATTHEW 13:31-32; MARK 4:30-32; AND LUKE 13:18-19.

It's a whole new mustard seed story! I want us to look at a couple of similarities in the stories written down by these three men. There were certain phrases that stuck out to the writers as they heard Jesus speak—let's look at those.

He presented another parable to them: "The kingdom of heaven is like a mustard seed that a man took and sowed in his field. It's the smallest of all the seeds, but when grown, it's taller than the vegetables and becomes a tree, so that the birds of the sky come and nest in its branches."
MATTHEW 13:31-32 (HCSB)

And He said: "How can we illustrate the kingdom of God, or what parable can we use to describe it? It's like a mustard seed that, when sown in the soil, is smaller than all the seeds on the ground. And when sown, it comes up and grows taller than all the vegetables, and produces large branches, so that the birds of the sky can nest in its shade."
MARK 4:30-32 (HCSB)

He said, therefore, "What is the kingdom of God like, and what can I compare it to? It's like a mustard seed that a man took and sowed in his garden. It grew and became a tree, and the birds of the sky nested in its branches."
LUKE 13:18-19 (HCSB)

Looking at all three passages of the same story, go back and circle these words:

kingdom	birds	sowed/sown
mustard seed	branches	nest/nested

These are the similarities in every story.

In Matthew and Mark, how is a mustard seed described?

LET'S LOOK AT ROMANS 5:3 AGAIN.

What part of this parable would correlate with each part of Romans 5:3? (match them!)

suffering   the birds nesting
perseverance   the seed being planted
character   the branches growing
hope   waiting for the seed to grow

Amazing, right? The model for us embracing perseverance is woven into nature! As the seed goes in the ground, it's covered in darkness and dirt.

Is there a situation in your life where you feel like you're surrounded by darkness? How would it change you if you thought of it more like you're a seed buried for growth?

Then the farmer waits. He has planted the seed, and now he must sit through multiple seasons.

How big does this plant grow (Matthew and Mark both mention it)?

Right. Taller than all the others. So the wait is probably long as the branches start to grow.

Compare the growth of a person's character to the growth of a plant's branches.

And then the birds nest. There's hope for them to cool off in the shade of the mustard plant.

It's the little things that make a big difference. "Big doors swing on small hinges" is a quote I have heard often. And in this story, that's proved true. A tiny seed, a little idea, a small contribution, given time and proper planting, grows into more than you could ever imagine.

That's how it is with the kingdom of God, right? It started out small, insignificant in the eyes of the world, but it grew exponentially. I think of a watermelon and a watermelon seed. It's hard to tell just by looking at that little seed that a full fruit could come from it. I think that's an interesting visual, just like the mustard seed to a tree, just like the kingdom of God.

What's the significance to you of birds nesting in the branches?

For me, the birds represent hope. The mustard seed has endured the dirt, the rain, and the growing. It has become big enough for a bird to make its home in the branches of what used to be a tiny seed. I picture the bird singing from the branch of a mustard seed and it reminds me that whatever I'm enduring, whatever I'm not quitting, will eventually lead to hope. Romans 5 tells me that.

> Not only so, but we also glory in our sufferings, because we know that suffering produces perseverance; perseverance, character; and character, hope. And hope does not put us to shame, because God's love has been poured out into our hearts through the Holy Spirit, who has been given to us.
> ROMANS 5:3-5

Farming requires patience, but even for the smallest of seeds, what grows when we allow the seasons to pass and when we trust the One who waters the plants and makes them grow is always worth it.

DAY 3
THE HIDDEN TREASURE

I'm a girl who loves fun. I'm almost always going to look for it, find it, and participate in it. It's my favorite hobby and pastime. It can be a doughnut eating contest, a beautiful fireworks show, swimming in a creek, or homemade hot chocolate and Christmas movies. I absolutely love having fun. No matter what it involves, I want to look for the lovely.

Recently, while speaking at a retreat in Michigan, the host informed us that just a few miles away were massive sand dunes. Immediately, I wanted to find them, to seek out the adventure. I wanted to climb them and see Lake Michigan on the other side.

Perseverance is often what I need most in moments like that. When the fun view is on the other side of an 80-degree-climb up a wall of sand, I need to remember what's on the other side, and I need that extra thing in me that says to keep going, knowing the top of the dunes will be worth the work it will take to get there.

READ JAMES 1:2-4.

Why must perseverance finish its work?

What would happen if a farmer quit his or her farm before the vegetables had grown?

Perseverance must finish its work in the garden, under the soil, in the darkness. The farmer has to trust and wait and watch for the mature fruit to develop.

I may have figured out one of the tricks to making it all the way to the end, to the place where there's hope, where the birds can rest on the branches, to the very spot where you're so glad you didn't throw in the towel when things felt hard, because now you're *here,* at the top of the sand dunes or holding a basket full of ripe fruit—anywhere there's hope.

Here's the trick: collect moments as you go, lovely moments with people you love, doing things you love, reading words you love, participating in a hobby you love, and treasure them. Now, they may not all happen at the same time, but identifying and having open eyes to the good God has given you will change your view every time. Hold on to those moments as you collect them. They are precious and valuable. Each of those moments can become energy to press on and not give up when difficulty inevitably comes.

As I was preparing and writing down my own journey of looking for lovely, I decided I wanted an actual jar, just as a little reminder of some moments that I want to put all in the same place, particularly the ones I've written about. So I got a mason jar and added in a picture of friends, a leaf from my favorite walking trial, and other things to symbolize the loveliness in my life. I collected moments literally and tangibly, and that jar reminds me to keep looking for the lovely every day.

> The kingdom of heaven is like treasure hidden in a field.
> When a man found it, he hid it again, and then in his joy
> went and sold all he had and bought that field.
> MATTHEW 13:44

Matthew is the only disciple who recorded this parable.

READ MATTHEW 9:9-13.

Where did Jesus find Matthew? What kind of guys did Matthew hang out with?

Why do you think the parable of the hidden treasure stood out to him?

It's interesting to note that it wasn't until Matthew 9 that Matthew wrote of his own opportunity to meet Jesus. I love that he just slid that in there: "Oh yeah, Jesus healed a paralyzed guy right before He walked over to the tax collector's booth and told me to leave my job and follow Him."

Matthew was a tax collector—he understood and probably liked to talk about and work with money—so this parable about a field, a treasure, and cost mattered to him.

The story matters to me (and we'll talk more about that later), but the author matters to me, too. Matthew probably wasn't a farmer since he was a tax collector, but he understood the culture and he certainly understood something valuable, something worth keeping.

GO BACK AND READ MATTHEW 13:44 AGAIN.

Why did the man hide the treasure after he found it?

Why did he sell everything he had? What does this verse say about the mood he was in when he sold everything?

There was something about that treasure. There was something about what he found in that field that changed that man's life. There was something in that field worth holding on to—enough so, that he sold all he had, *with joy,* to buy the field. The Greek transliteration of *treasure* is *thēsauros.*

> *thēsauros* (noun) — (1) the place in which good and precious things are collected and laid up: a receptacle, in which valuables are kept; a treasury; storehouse; (2) collected treasures[1]

This is the same original word, *treasure*, that Matthew used in Matthew 6.

READ MATTHEW 6:20-21.

Putting this verse with the parable, what does that say about the man's heart?

When it comes to perseverance, I think it's a matter of the heart. It's not my body that wants to quit; it's often my mind. Climbing up that sand dune, I definitely felt my body tiring and my legs wearing down. I also heard whispers in my mind that it wasn't going to be worth it, that I was running out of time to be back at the retreat center, that the hill may just be too steep and too challenging to reach the top.

Then I think about my friend and how we have taken jumping pictures together at the top. I remember the times I've hiked when the view was totally worth the climb. I relive how much I love seeing the view over Lake Michigan.

And I keep going.

It took me thinking about those treasures, the things that matter most to me—it took looking for lovely even in the pain—and that's why I was able to finish, climb to the top, and take some great pictures in a sea of sand in the middle of Michigan.

What kind of treasure do you think Jesus is referring to in Matthew 6:21?

Jesus isn't talking about things at all. He says we need to store our treasures in heaven. The treasures we store in heaven are all spiritual things—obedience, character, grace, spiritual fruit, hope. These are the things we should treasure.

How do we store up spiritual treasures, treasures in heaven?

This is not as easy as finding earthly treasures. We must learn to look for lovely in God's promises, in the people He sends us to love and tell about Him, in the ways He asks us to trust Him. When we truly treasure these things, we will do anything to get them. What we treasure is displayed in our actions. When we treasure earthly things, it will be evident by the way we live our lives.

READ MATTHEW 13:44 AGAIN.

Why purchase the entire field instead of just taking the thing he found?

Have you ever wanted something so much that you would pay any price for it? Journal about your experience.

This man found treasure. He found something that he would do anything to obtain. His actions declared where his treasure was found.

What do your actions reveal that you treasure?

1. *"thēsauros,"* Blue Letter Bible, Strong's 2344. Available online at *blueletterbible.org*.

DAY 4
FARMERS DON'T QUIT

Driving from Nashville, Tennessee, to South Georgia, I listened to a podcast sermon from a friend of mine. Mark was teaching on patience, which has to go hand in hand with seasons of perseverance. As I'm driving and listening, I'm nodding along and saying "Mmhmm" and "Yes, sir!" in agreement. And then he starts talking about farmers, and my ears perk up in a new way.

"Look at the farmer. Look how he does it. He's patient until he receives the early and late rains,"[1] he said. "They are constantly working while they're waiting."[2]

Mind. Blown.

Again, because I live around the 98 percent of Americans who aren't full-time farmers, this just isn't something I had thought about. Farmers live in the season that's happening, but they're always planning for the next season and celebrating the season that has passed.

But they don't spend days sitting and wondering if their crop is going to grow.

READ ECCLESIASTES 3:1-13.

In verse 1, it says there's a time or season for every what?

Some Bible versions say "activity." Others say "matter," "event," or "purpose," but all of those are action words. None of them are waiting words. There are seasons for every activity—rest, action, and everything in between.

Farmers never quit. Farmers rest, but they never quit. As it says in Ecclesiastes, "there is a time for everything." To me, that means there's always an action, always a choice. Every season offers its unique experience, if we choose, like a farmer, to see what needs to be done—between sowing and reaping—but never quitting.

But it's not just for farmers. We can't quit either. We must trust in the knowledge that another season is coming; we can believe that God is working even when we don't see it. Farmers tend the land, farmers harvest the produce, farmers pray for the soil, but they don't sit at home, fingers crossed that all the things in the field will just work out.

The Bible is full of reminders for us to keep at it, to finish the season strong and prepare for the next one. Because it's worth it.

READ ROMANS 5:3-4 AGAIN.

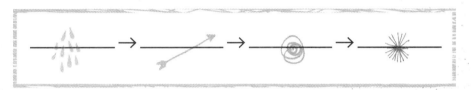

The suffering is worth it for the farmer—the hot days in the sun, the care for the seeds, the protection of the soil—for the hope of the vegetable to grow on the other side of the work.

I keep Bible study books like this one you're holding on the bottom shelf of the bookcase in my living room. At times, the Lord will remind me of something I've studied or read that I want to read again. I want this page to be that for you, friend.

I want to have a farmer's heart when it comes to how I face the trials in my life, the seasons of waiting, and the harder-than-I-realized times.

I want to find purpose and joy in the sowing seasons. I'm quick to label those seasons as "too busy" or "stressful." But the sowing is not hard labor with no return, even though the results may not be immediate. I want to find the same amount of purpose in a cold winter struggle at the gym or working on my computer as I do in the warm summer, when I look around and see so much harvest in my relationships, my health, and my career. I've asked God for a heart that appreciates all the seasons, when I can find gratefulness in both the struggle and in the reward. I've prayed for a heart that waits well, works hard, and perseveres, happily walking through the doors God opens for me.

I also want that for you.

Let's dig into a few places in the Bible where we're reminded never to give up, to keep going, to press on and press in, and to grow.

But we have this treasure in jars of clay to show that this
all-surpassing power is from God and not from us. We are hard
pressed on every side, but not crushed; perplexed, but not in despair;
persecuted, but not abandoned; struck down, but not destroyed.
2 CORINTHIANS 4:7-9

Describe a time in your life when you felt hard-pressed.

What kept you from being "destroyed" (v. 9)?

READ 2 CORINTHIANS 4:16-18.

What's one way not to lose heart (think of yesterday's study)?

What should we focus on instead of our current pain (check out vv. 14-15)? Why?

Phew. Perseverance pays off in the growth of your character and in the gift of hope. Yet we can't do it on our own—it's not up to you to "man up" through your trials in order to gain perseverance, character, and hope.

So neither the one who plants nor the one who waters is
anything, but only God, who makes things grow.
1 CORINTHIANS 3:7

What does this verse mean to you when you think about seasons and sowing and the work of a farmer?

In its context, Paul was talking about the growth of the church and discipleship. What can we learn from this Scripture about God's role in everything that's planted and grows?

Only God.

Only God can get you through the hard times. Only God can give you the persevering heart of a farmer. Only God can grow in you the things you need. Only God.

So as you pursue a life where you collect the moments that help you persevere, remember only God can make fruit grow in your life.

Journal a prayer to God, asking for a farmer's heart.

1. Mark Fritchman, *20150719 – Give Me Patience... Now!* Podcast audio. MP3, 23:41-47. Accessed March 7, 2016. Available online at *http://www.sscommunitychurch.com/20150719-give-me-patience-now-mark-fritchman/*.
2. Mark Fritchman, *20150719 – Give Me Patience... Now!* Podcast audio. MP3, 22:30-33. Accessed March 7, 2016. Available online at *http://www.sscommunitychurch.com/20150719-give-me-patience-now-mark-fritchman/*.

Session 3

MUSICIANS

I love living in Nashville. I've long been a fan of country music and a well-placed banjo, and Nashville never disappoints.

I grew up playing music. I love to sing (trust me, I love to sing more than you love for me to sing), but I'm a harmony girl. I love knowing all the parts of a song and singing the alto harmony. I taught myself to play piano using a tiny laptop keyboard and a hymnal that my third grade choir director gave me. I played the French horn in middle school, and I taught myself guitar using YouTube when I was in college.

There isn't an instrument that I wouldn't enjoy learning to play.

Yet, as you can imagine, I'm a novice at them all. I know the basics—the right things to push, the way to read notes—but I'm no expert. What I can do is technical, not beautiful. I will tell you, without shame, I don't think it's a lack of ability. I think I could have been good, maybe really good, at any of those instruments.

I often wish I would've continued to play the French horn. I loved it. I loved the sound; I loved the place it holds in an orchestra. It's the instrumental version of what I like to sing—the subtle but important alto line. I can barely watch a band or symphony without just kicking myself for quitting.

But the ones who don't quit? The experts? The professionals? What they do is absolutely beautiful. Nashville is full of those types of musicians—the ones who put in the hours of practice and the years of hard work to be the best in their field.

There's something about singing, something about making music, that brings lovely into our lives. It's not just hearing it, though hearing it can change your life as well. It's the making of it. It's the participation in the creation that God calls us to.

GROUP GUIDE

WELCOME!

Before you begin discussing this session's personal study, talk as a group about what you've found during this study as you've looked for lovely. What lovely things have crossed your path? If you haven't already, go ahead and read the session introduction on the previous page together as a group.

AS WE BEGIN, DISCUSS THE FOLLOWING QUESTIONS WITH YOUR GROUP:

How do we continually plant seeds of God's Word in our lives?

Do your actions show what you treasure? How so?

Describe a time in your life when you felt hard-pressed.

WATCH THE VIDEO:

To hear more from Annie, download the optional teen girls' video bundle to view Session 3 at *lifeway.com/girls.*

NOW, LET'S TALK:

Read Daniel 2:20-21a. What does it mean that God changes the seasons?

How do we appreciate the season we're in? How do we prepare for new seasons of life?

What role does looking for lovely play in season change?

What's your favorite kind of music? Favorite bands? Favorite song?

PRAY:

Pray together, thanking God for His Word. Thank Him for the treasure of the gospel. Thank Him for seasons in our lives. Ask Him to help you learn to sing in all seasons, looking for lovely along the way.

DAY 1
DAVID

Probably the most famous musician in the Bible is King David. The writer of the majority of the Psalms, King David, was a singer/songwriter who used his ability to write poetry and play musical instruments. Sounds like he would fit perfectly in Nashville, huh?

But David didn't pick up the guitar at sixty years old, and he didn't practice once a month as a kid. Even when we're young, either in years or in faith, practice matters. Practice is what perseverance is all about.

When you think of David, you probably pretty quickly think of Goliath too (see 1 Sam. 17). But before the giant got a stone to the forehead, David was already known by King Saul, and it had to do with his musical talent.

READ FROM 1 SAMUEL 16 BELOW.

Now the Spirit of the LORD had departed from Saul, and an evil spirit from the LORD tormented him. Saul's attendants said to him, "See, an evil spirit from God is tormenting you. Let our lord command his servants here to search for someone who can play the lyre. He will play when the evil spirit from God comes on you, and you will feel better." So Saul said to his attendants, "Find someone who plays well and bring him to me." One of the servants answered, "I have seen a son of Jesse of Bethlehem who knows how to play the lyre. He is a brave man and a warrior. He speaks well and is a fine-looking man. And the LORD is with him."

Then Saul sent messengers to Jesse and said, "Send me your son David, who is with the sheep." So Jesse took a donkey loaded with bread, a skin of wine and a young goat and sent them with his son David to Saul. David came to Saul and entered his service. Saul liked him very much, and David became one of his armor-bearers. Then Saul sent word to Jesse, saying, "Allow David to remain in my service, for I am pleased with him." Whenever the spirit from God came on Saul, David would take up his lyre and play. Then relief would come to Saul; he would feel better, and the evil spirit would leave him.
1 SAMUEL 16:14-23

The Spirit of the Lord had left Saul, leaving Saul exposed to torment by an evil spirit. Seeing him troubled and terrified, Saul's servants came up with an interesting solution. Their idea was to get a musician to play for Saul so he would feel better. Saul was also on board with the plan. He just asked that they find someone who could play well (1 Sam. 16:17). I'm all about this method of healing. I love a good playlist, and the right music can lift my mood and help calm my spirit.

How was David described to King Saul by the servant?

David seemed to meet the requirements Saul had for a musician, so he dispatched his servants to go and get David. One of my favorite parts of this account is in verse 19. When King Saul sent for David, he wasn't in the studio or practicing the harp in his family's living room. He was with the sheep. David was a shepherd.

What would happen to Saul when David would play his harp?

READ 1 SAMUEL 17:34-35.

Based on these passages, what do you think David's life was like when he was out in the fields with the sheep? What kinds of things might he have had with him?

This changes how I picture David's life as a young shepherd boy. He traveled with a harp, probably some rope, and some sort of weapon that kept him (and his sheep) safe from the lions and the bears.

I picture that as the sheep wandered around and munched on the grass, David sat on a rock, watching his flock, writing songs, and practicing his harp, and occasionally, you know, killing a massive predator.

And then, by 1 Samuel 16, David's skill on the harp was widely enough known that he was suggested as the best harpist around.

We can learn from David's life, even as a young man, even before the Goliath incident, about what music can do for a person—not only the player, but also the one listening.

How do you think music helped David? How did it help King Saul?

Think back to Romans 5:3-4. How did you see suffering, perseverance, character, and hope in Saul's and David's stories?

We see in Saul's life, as he suffered through the torment, that music soothed him.

What songs have done that for you?

David's practice paid off. We could talk for pages and pages about the psalms David wrote and how they turned his heart toward God, as well as others for many generations to come. A songwriter's job is to look for lovely, isn't it? If that artist is trying to write songs that bring hope, they're looking around the world in which they live, identifying the life-giving and beautiful, and writing honestly about their experiences with the beautiful in the world.

Which songwriters/musicians do you love? Which ones point you to hope?

I have a friend in Nashville who wrote a song about my life once. I didn't know it was about me, but the first time I heard it, I loved it. I thought, *Man, that song makes tons of sense and kind of expresses exactly what I am feeling!* He wove in some truth that spoke into a hard season I was experiencing. As I listened to it, it brought me hope. I asked him about it once, sheepishly, to see if the similarities to my life actually came from my life. And yep, they did.

I love the song so much. It reminds me of things I know about my own life but can forget at times, like I'm never alone. The song showed me what others see and feel when they live life with me—how my people experience pain and longing right alongside me. And it brought back to mind truths I needed to hear again—that I am loved by God and my friends. The songwriter looked for lovely in my life and found it. And when he found it, it helped me find it again too.

David does that to me in the Psalms as well. Though he clearly didn't know me when he penned his poems, it sometimes feels like David is speaking right to my heart.

¹ The LORD is my shepherd, I lack nothing.
² He makes me lie down in green pastures,
he leads me beside quiet waters,
³ he refreshes my soul.
He guides me along the right paths
for his name's sake.
⁴ Even though I walk
through the darkest valley,
I will fear no evil,
for you are with me;
your rod and your staff,
they comfort me.

⁵ You prepare a table before me
in the presence of my enemies.
You anoint my head with oil;
my cup overflows.
⁶ Surely your goodness and love will follow me
all the days of my life,
and I will dwell in the house of the LORD
forever.
PSALM 23

Which verse(s) brings you hope?

Maybe it's time for you to grab some new music or even expand your list of favorite musicians. Why not post on Facebook or Twitter to ask who your friends are listening to?

"I'm searching for some new tunes that are full of hope. Got a favorite you'd suggest? #lookingforlovely"

DAY 2
MIRIAM & MARY

I listen to music as I get ready every morning. My friend Christen taught me how to make playlists on my iTunes® (which makes me feel like an old woman to need tech help like that), and so I listen to my "get thee ready" list as I pry my eyes open and get my day moving.

Those songs, as my day goes by, always pop back into my head. I still sing them throughout my day. But the one by Housefires called "Good Good Father" comes back almost daily. I sing along to it in my mind (or out loud if there are no humans around).

Based on what's going on with my day, or in my heart, I take their melody and some of their words and add my own. Because sometimes I like to worship God through a song that's my own, and sometimes getting through a hard day or a hard moment is only possible when I bring my own lovely truth into it.

Do you ever do that?

When has a song stuck with you through your day?

There are two women in the Bible who wrote their own songs, Miriam and Mary, to bring hope to their own hearts and to mark where they were in their journeys. The songs are beautiful to read.

MIRIAM, MOSES' SISTER

READ EXODUS 15.

Who sang this song?

Miriam's song follows the song of her younger brother, Moses. As I read Exodus 15 again today, I have two verses underlined. I've had the same Bible since I was a freshman in high school, so I have no idea when I underlined these two particular statements. Yet even today as I reread them, they remind me of some beautiful truths I need.

> ² The LORD is my strength and my defense;
>   he has become my salvation.
>   He is my God, and I will praise him,
>   my father's God, and I will exalt him.
>
> ¹³ In your unfailing love you will lead
>   the people you have redeemed.
>   In your strength you will guide them
>   to your holy dwelling.
>
> EXODUS 15:2,13

Those are the two verses that stand out to me in Moses' song.

Which verse stands out to you? Why?

READ EXODUS 15:20-21 AGAIN.

After Moses sings an eighteen-verse song, along with all the people, Miriam steps in. It was a very big sister move. She seemed to often be close by, ready to help Moses when he needed her. In fact, the first time we see their relationship is when Moses is an infant.

READ EXODUS 2:1-10.

What was Miriam's role in Moses' survival as a baby?

By the time we get to Exodus 15, Moses is leading the Israelites away from their captivity in Egypt, and his siblings—Aaron and Miriam—are along at every step.

What did Miriam add to Moses' song? Why do you think she wanted to sing that statement to the women and the ones listening? What was she instructing them to do?

READ EXODUS 15:22-24.

What happens immediately after the song?

Finding the lovely in a moment, recognizing God's provision when things are still challenging and hard, and worshiping through it all, makes all the difference. Miriam wrote her own song, reminding the people how God cares for them, not knowing that three days without water was on the way.

This is all speculation, but I bet Miriam kept singing this song over and over for the next few days, as things seemed to get more difficult for her, Moses, and the people of Israel.

Last night, after a tough day and then a long walk at my favorite place, Radnor Lake, I swung by the store to grab a few groceries. I noticed, as I was walking around, that the song from my walk was still resounding in my head. The lyrics of "What a Saviour" from Hillsong Worship walked with me all day long, reminding me of what's true, even when I don't feel it.

What songs have meant a lot to you during difficult times in your life?

MARY, THE MOTHER OF JESUS

Mary sang a song as well. And much like Miriam, she sang in the middle—months after finding out she was pregnant and prior to Jesus' birth.

READ LUKE 1:39-56.

In this passage, Mary visited her relative, Elizabeth. We know from earlier in the chapter that Elizabeth was also miraculously pregnant with John the Baptist.

What did Elizabeth say to Mary? Why do you think that inspired Mary to sing?

Think about the situation Mary was in. She was young, unmarried, and pregnant. She had heard from an angel that she would give birth to God's Son. Can you imagine? She sings this song in the middle of being unsure of her future.

Why is it significant that Mary sang these words in the middle of what she was walking through? How do you think they helped her to persevere?

It's always hard for me to sing from the middle. Sing at the start? I can do that. Because at the start I'm so full of hope and excitement and WOOHOO! Sing at the end? Yes, please. We made it, the race is over; I knew we'd be fine—let's celebrate! But in the middle? When things seem hard and unsure and you don't totally know where it's going? You gotta sing from there. You have to persevere there, let your worship build character in you.

I see that in me. Whether it's because I'm sad, lonely, or afraid, I see in me times when I don't want to sing the songs that are on the screen at church. It takes me mustering up some courage to say some of the lyrics that feel hard to believe. And every time I sing them, I believe a little more. It grows my character and causes just a little muscle growth in my soul. Even if I'm smack in the middle, if I'll sing true things to God about God, it helps me hang on.

What's a situation where you're right in the middle, like Miriam and Mary?

I'm going to ask you to do a little something crazy. Pick your favorite worship song and let it start playing in the background. Maybe it's something new and modern or maybe it's an old hymn, but just start playing it.

As you're thinking about the situation you listed above, start writing down some words of worship that come to mind—who you know God is and what you know is true about Him, even in the middle.

DAY 3
PAUL & SILAS

Our church does a really excellent job of teaching us new songs. If I've got their system figured out, I think they intro a new song at the end of a service, bring it into the worship set the next week, and then take a week off. Then they put the song in the worship set for two more weeks solid and then rotate it in and out. By the third exposure, I've pretty much got it. (Or at least that's what I tell myself.)

I remember the first time I bought a CD of worship music. I was at a summer camp for a week and the band leading worship also had CDs to sell. I couldn't believe it! I could listen to the songs that we were doing from stage anytime I wanted!

I know. That sounds ridiculous now in a world where we can hear a song, open our phones, and own it ten seconds later. But at the time, it felt like such a miracle that I could have, in my personal possession, the worship songs we sang at church. Now, even as I'm typing this, music from one of my favorite worship groups is playing for me in the background. It's the middle of the night as I write and the music is keeping me going.

In Acts, we read a story about Paul and Silas and their worship. I wonder what they sang—was it a song they already knew? One that had been sung at the gatherings of those who followed Christ? Or was it a song they made up, sitting there together? Music soothes in the darkness, and as we'll see today, it can also usher in freedom.

READ ACTS 16:16-21.

Why were Paul and Silas arrested (vv. 20-21)?

Why were the owners actually angry (v. 19)?

READ ACTS 16:22-24.

Describe Paul and Silas' condition.

These men weren't just tossed in a jail cell like in a cartoon where the cell slams shut but the silly sheriff forgets to lock the door. They were beaten, flogged, bloody, and in pain. Their feet were in shackles, and it must have been so dark and dank in that inner cell. Gross.

> About midnight Paul and Silas were praying and singing hymns to God, and the other prisoners were listening to them. Suddenly there was such a violent earthquake that the foundations of the prison were shaken. At once all the prison doors flew open, and everyone's chains came loose.
> ACTS 16:25-26

What time was it when Paul and Silas were singing and praying? What were the other prisoners doing when Paul and Silas sang?

An important first thing to note—it was at about midnight. About midnight Paul and Silas were praying and singing hymns to God.

How would you describe what it would be like at midnight in a first-century prison?

There's nothing lovely about being in a first-century prison, especially in the middle of the night. And yet, Paul and Silas were praying and singing.

I think about midnights in my own life. I haven't been in a literal first-century prison, but there have been times when I've felt beaten down and imprisoned, times when I haven't been able to find the lovely in my circumstances. I bet you've been there too. The beauty of this story is that, even at midnight, Paul and Silas were singing.

What makes you sing during the midnights in your life?

We don't know what Paul and Silas were singing. We don't know what they were saying in their prayers to God. What I love about this story is that they didn't need to see lovely in their circumstances. They knew they could find lovely in their God.

When we worship, we look straight at Jesus. Yes, worship is a lifestyle—it's the way we live our everyday life. But in this case, it looked like singing and praying. And when we sing about God, we can't help but focus on Him. We look away from our circumstances and toward Him. Like the words of a very old church song, when we "Turn Your Eyes upon Jesus," the things of this world fade away.[1]

I mean, they don't disappear, right? I'm not trying to paint an unrealistic picture. Your troubles don't always leave, but their power fades. Because the beauty is too much for it. Looking at Jesus, worshiping Him, puts your eyes on His ability instead of on the cell around you or the chains on your feet. And sometimes, when you're persevering through the suffering, letting it build your character and bring hope, worship is also the key that unlocks your cell door.

> The jailer woke up, and when he saw the prison doors open, he drew his sword and was about to kill himself because he thought the prisoners had escaped. But Paul shouted, "Don't harm yourself! We are all here!"
> ACTS 16:27-28

What happened as Paul and Silas were singing? What was the jailer's initial reaction?

The prisoners had the chance to go free. The earthquake loosened their chains and the prison door opened. We don't know why they didn't move, but we know that they showed integrity in staying put. We don't know how many other prisoners were housed with Paul and Silas, and we don't know if they became believers that night. We only know they stayed.

The jailer called for lights, rushed in and fell trembling before Paul and Silas. He then brought them out and asked, "Sirs, what must I do to be saved?" They replied, "Believe in the Lord Jesus, and you will be saved—you and your household." Then they spoke the word of the Lord to him and to all the others in his house. At that hour of the night the jailer took them and washed their wounds; then immediately he and all his household were baptized. The jailer brought them into his house and set a meal before them; he was filled with joy because he had come to believe in God—he and his whole household.

ACTS 16:29-34

The prisoners stayed in prison, and the jailer came to saving faith in Jesus Christ as a direct result of the faithfulness of Paul and Silas. They were faithful to preach the gospel, faithful to sing through midnight, and faithful to share Jesus with the jailer.

When we look for lovely even in the most difficult situations, people around us notice. We collect moments of God's goodness and faithfulness so that when we're imprisoned and in dark situations, we can remember the loveliness of God. We can remember that He is faithful, no matter what. And we can praise Him in our midnights.

I've been trying to memorize Psalm 51, one or two verses at a time. It's an important psalm to me, especially because I'm a sinner. (I'm sure you understand, being that we all are.) Sometimes my sin feels like a jail cell, and only God's forgiveness can get me out.

READ PSALM 51.

Maybe, just tonight, you stay up until that clock hits midnight. Open to Psalm 51 in your Bible. Take a minute to experience the dark that is midnight, even in your home. No candles, no lights, just for a couple of minutes, sit in the absolute dark of midnight.

And then, click on a light, or plug in a string of twinkly lights. Start playing your favorite worship song. And then pray. Pray and worship, like Paul and Silas. If you want, write out prayers for people you know who need freedom. And pray that as you worship, their chains will fall off, too.

1. The words to "Turn Your Eyes upon Jesus" were written by Helen H. Lemmel. You can read them in the *Baptist Hymnal* (Nashville, TN: LifeWay Worship, 2008), 413:

DAY 4
FEATHERS

When I was in college, I worked for Athens Janitor Supply Company. Yes, it's actually what you think—a company that provides janitorial supplies. My job every day is a little difficult to explain, but I'll try. You see, every product that the company sold had to have a MSDS— Material Safety Data Sheet. It's simply a piece of paper that tells the hazards of the product. So my job that summer was to make sure every MSDS sheet was accounted for, scanned into the system, and then filed in alphabetical order.

I didn't have an office—I had a cubicle in the corner of the conference room. So every day at lunch, a coworker named Jerry would come and sit in the room and eat his sandwich. Jerry was probably in his mid-50s and was a super nice guy. We would chat for a minute, but then he would get to work memorizing chapters of the Bible. *Chapters.* I had never seen such a thing. But I would listen to him practice, amazed at what he could remember.

I finally asked him about it one day. He told me all the benefits of memorizing a chapter and how to do it. And then he told me where to start: Psalm 103.

READ PSALM 103.

Call me crazy, but I'd love for you to copy the entire psalm in your journal or somewhere you will see it often.

I thought it would be impossible. No way would I ever be able to remember that much Scripture. But when you learn one or two verses a day, repeating them daily—perhaps even working on them during your lunch break—it's actually doable. And it did exactly what Jerry said it would—it made my mind focus on praising God for all the things He does for me, versus finding lots of reasons to worry or complain.

Which verse of Psalm 103 stands out most to you? Why?

Years later, I can still almost quote all of Psalm 103 to you without looking.
I just practiced and got stumped a few times, but to be fair—it has been awhile.

I absolutely love the first five verses. I love the reminders of who God is and why we should worship Him.

> In verses 3-5, David lists five of God's "benefits" (as they are called in
> v. 2). What are they?

Each one is important. And when we're building a life where we worship on purpose, where we look for lovely, where we sing to God even when it doesn't feel good, then these benefits are what we need to remember.

> Fill in the blank for each of the benefits below by describing how it
> actually affects your life and what happens as a result. For example: If
> God forgives all my sins, then I can forgive others.
>
> If God forgives all my sins, then _____
>
> _____
>
> _____
>
> If God heals all my diseases, then _____
>
> _____
>
> _____
>
> If God redeems my life from the pit, then _____
>
> _____
>
> _____

If God crowns me with love and compassion, then _____

_____

_____.

If God satisfies my desires with good things, then _____

_____

_____.

What does it mean that "your youth is renewed like the eagle's" (v. 5)?

If the culmination of singing and praising the Lord with my soul and remembering His benefits means that my youth is renewed, what does that look like for your everyday life?

Is true worship actually the fountain of youth? Is there something that happens when we worship that makes us stronger, like when we were younger?

In reading the original Hebrew of Psalm 103:5 (thanks to commentaries, obviously, not my own personal ability to read Hebrew), it says that this renewal is like when an eagle is molting.

> *chadash* [sounds like *khaw-dash'*] (verb) — a primitive root; to be new; causatively, to rebuild: renew, repair[1]

When eagles molt, they have to give up their feathers, because as they fly, fish, and nest, their feathers become heavy from being covered in dirt and oil. When they molt, the old feathers fall out and fresh new ones replace the old, allowing for better flying, soaring, and protection.

Isn't that kind of like what happened to Paul and Silas? They worshiped and the things holding them back fell off. Isn't it similar to Mary? Wasn't David's worship before King Saul a way to remove the pain from the king?

I've been blown away by this. I think it's true in my life—the more I worship, the more I find beauty in Him, the more the things that bring me down molt off and are renewed in Christ. Wow, the things of this world do fade away, don't they?

Today, I'm thinking of three situations where I could really use some molting. I have some financial worries that are causing stress in decision making. I just want to shake off the worries. My best friend just started dating a guy and suddenly my head is filled with, *You're always going to be alone; it will never be your turn;* and *why doesn't God answer my prayers?* kind of thoughts. Mucky, gross feathers for sure. I also have a friendship that's struggling—there was a misunderstanding and for some reason I just can't get over it. It feels weird and bad, and it makes me feel sadness.

It's not that I want the people involved in these situations to be removed—it's just places where I'm suffering a little, struggling a lot, and asking God what's going on. And it feels like they're bringing me down a bit. (Again, *not* the humans, just the situations and my worries.)

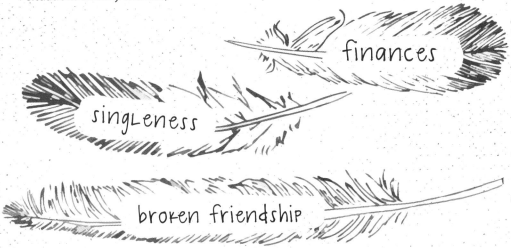

Those are the three feathers I want to see molt for me—to change my view. I want to see God more clearly, to hear His voice really well, and to learn and grow from the molting process. I want God to equip me to handle the experiences with grace and love, like Jesus.

Yet even in the molting process, the situations may not get better immediately. If we look back to the stories we discussed this session, Miriam headed straight into a desert after singing her song. Mary was still young and pregnant. King Saul eventually tried to hunt David down to kill him, and Paul and Silas didn't know if they'd ever get out of that prison.

Here are your three feathers. What situations come to mind where if focused on God, looking at His benefits, you would hope the things of this world would fade away?

What Psalm 103 tells us is that the feathers that hold us down, from sin or the muck of painful situations, those will molt off as we focus on God's benefits, as we worship Him. We'll feel lighter, younger, full of life. Maybe you will still have cancer or you will not make the team. But the molting is more about perspective. You won't be weighed down by worry, by anger. Your sin is forgiven. You are made whole in Christ.

I'm still single. My finances still cause some worries. My friendship still needs healing.

But I'm lighter. And as I worship, I just believe that the molting will continue until all that so easily entangles and holds me back will float off me like feathers from an eagle.

I'm believing God for that in my life. And in yours.

1. *"chadash,"* Blue Letter Bible, Strong's 2318. Available online at *blueletterbible.org*.

FISHING

I grew up in a house beside a pond. We call it a lake, but that's a huge compliment to the actual size of the man-made water feature. It's a pond. You can walk the full circumference in about 20 minutes if you're meandering.

About once a week during my growing up summers, dad would take us fishing in our little tin boat with our life vests on. We would sing all sorts of songs. I love fishing. It's thoughtful and quiet and repetitive. It's a little calculated and scientific if you're an aficionado (a-FISH-ionado, am I right?!?) or a true sportsman, but for me as a nine-year-old, it was just a hobby and time with my dad. We caught a few every time, cooked them sometimes, and threw them back more often than not. We weren't trying to live off the land or anything, just fishing for fun.

But the people who do it professionally? The ones who are legit fishermen? They have a lot to think about. Weather. Location. Tools. Life jackets.

Jesus loved to hang out with fishermen, mostly along the shores of the Sea of Galilee. We see it throughout the Gospels—those dudes were interesting to Jesus. He spoke their language and understood their lives.

I've swum in the Sea of Galilee. The water is smooth and thick, like lake water, but it's salty. The bottom is muddy and you can sink to your ankles if you stand in one spot too long. The shore is made up of fist-sized rocks that seriously hurt the bottom of your feet as you hobble to the sand. And the fish. Y'all. They swim around your back and between your knees and in every direction. As I paddled around the sea with my friends, I thought about Peter and John and the other fisherman Jesus met, right there on that shore. These men were the ones who knew the fish types that swam in the Sea of Galilee and the ones who knew what the muddy sea bottom felt like between their toes.

I've spent a lot of time reading about the fishermen in the Bible, wondering what it looked like for them to collect moments, to find the beauty in their everyday in a way that encouraged them to fish through the night. And I kept going back to one thing— the nets.

GROUP GUIDE

WELCOME!
Before you begin discussing this session's personal study, talk as a group about what you've found during this study as you've looked for lovely. What lovely things have crossed your path? If you haven't already, go ahead and read the session introduction on the previous page together as a group.

AS WE BEGIN, DISCUSS THE FOLLOWING QUESTIONS WITH YOUR GROUP:
Read Psalm 23. What part of this passage brings you hope?

What makes you sing during the midnights in your life?

Would you be brave enough to share your feathers from Day 4? Pray for each other after discussing them.

WATCH THE VIDEO:
To hear more from Annie, download the optional teen girls' video bundle to view Session 4 at *lifeway.com/girls.*

NOW, LET'S TALK:
Do you have a place that marks God's faithfulness for you? Tell the group about it.

Read John 21:1-3. Why do you think the disciples returned to the Sea of Galilee? What did that place mean to them?

What experience do you have fishing? How do you think fishermen look for lovely?

PRAY:
Pray together, thanking God for music, especially the music recorded in His Word. Ask Him to teach you this session to become even more avid collectors of His loveliness.

DAY 1
AMPHIBLĒSTRON

We have to be collectors. We have to look around our lives and store up the sweet moments, the profound, and the simple—the ones that help us to hold on and let our character build as we persevere. As I told you, I keep reminders of these moments in a jar. I have a collection of lovely things to remind me of God's goodness and faithfulness for when times are difficult.

Jesus walked up to a bunch of collectors early in the Gospel of Matthew.

LOOK AT MATTHEW 4:1-17.

What happens first in this chapter?

So, this is the very beginning of Jesus' ministry. Right after He is tempted by the Devil, Jesus begins to preach and heads out to meet the first men He'll ask to be His disciples.

> As Jesus was walking beside the Sea of Galilee, he saw two brothers, Simon called Peter and his brother Andrew. They were casting a net into the lake, for they were fishermen. "Come, follow me," Jesus said, "and I will send you out to fish for people." At once they left their nets and followed him.
> MATTHEW 4:18-20

Where was Jesus walking? What two men did He find first?

Using the context clues, do you think Simon and Andrew were fishing from a boat or in the shallow part of the sea? Why?

Matthew used a specific word here to tell us what kind of net these men were using to fish with. The particular type of net is only mentioned twice in the Bible—here and in Mark 1:16 (which tells the exact same story of Simon and Andrew).

From *Trench's New Testament Synonyms:*

> The *amphiblēstron* is a casting net. When skillfully cast from the shore or over the shoulder from a boat, this net spreads out into a circle as it falls on the water, where it sinks swiftly because of its lead weights and encloses whatever is below it. Its circular, bell-like shape made it suitable for use as a mosquito net.[1]

The way this particular net works, the one that Simon and Andrew were using when Jesus saw them, is that when the fisherman sees movement below him—whether in a boat, on the shoreline, or standing in shallow water—he throws the net out and it sinks around the fish and hopefully others from the same school.[2]

This net can only be used in the daytime successfully.[3]

Why do you think that is?

You're gonna have to get behind me on this, but I think we can collect moments like Simon and Andrew collected fish. Simply, every day, eyes open, net in hand.

The fishermen in Jesus' time worked with eyes wide open to little glimmers of hope. The *amphiblēstron* net is held in the hands of the fishermen and used where they can physically see the fish. The edges of the nets are weighted so that when the net is thrown in the water, it will sink to the bottom, catching everything in that area. The fisherman then tightens the string he never threw out, and it gathers together the edges of the net, closing it in on the fish in the middle.

Knowing this, we can guess the disciples used this method of fishing, too. They probably didn't just throw the net haphazardly, tossing it out and bringing it in over and over all day long. I imagine they would stand still and quiet in the more shallow parts of the Sea of Galilee, with its rocky and muddy bottom, and watch intently. When they saw a shimmering fish swim by, they knew there were probably more around. So that would be the cue to throw the net, hoping that by seeing one fish and trying to catch it, they would run into an entire school.[4]

When I picture *amphiblēstron,* I picture the things that happen in our everyday lives. I imagine this as our daily moments of gratefulness. This kind of net is the one we keep close to us. And when we notice one good thing, we toss the net to catch it and notice more blessings, gifts, and moments than we realized were right in front of us all along.

What these men needed, and what we need, are eyes to see.

> Taste and see that the LORD is good;
> blessed is the one who takes refuge in him.
> **PSALM 34:8**

We are given two instructions in that first line:

Taste and _____...

We have to choose to have eyes that see the everyday moments around us that are worth holding on to—to see that God is good. And every time their nets came up with fish? It reminded them not to quit fishing. The hard days and the empty net times were worth it, because sometimes the nets were full—they found the lovely when they looked for it, right there, flopping around in their nets.

> I keep asking that the God of our Lord Jesus Christ, the glorious
> Father, may give you the Spirit of wisdom and revelation, so that
> you may know him better. I pray that the eyes of your heart may be
> enlightened in order that you may know the hope to which he has
> called you, the riches of his glorious inheritance in his holy people, and
> his incomparably great power for us who believe. That power is the
> same as the mighty strength he exerted when he raised Christ from
> the dead and seated him at his right hand in the heavenly realms
> **EPHESIANS 1:17-20**

What's Paul praying for his friends in Ephesus?

I've been working out with a trainer once a week or so because I want my arms to be stronger. I have to lift lots of boxes of books and suitcases, and I'm tired of looking like a wimp in the airport. Well, last week, I lifted a suitcase and assured myself it was light enough to fly because of how easy it was for me to lift. And sure enough, I got to the airport and it was more than 50 pounds. At first, I was super annoyed, but then I realized, "hey, this is a little fish swimming right below me"—a little reminder that perseverance paid off—consistently lifting weights has actually made me stronger. So instead of feeling frustrated that I had to put a pair of shoes in my carry-on and wear an extra sweater, I was grateful that I am getting stronger.

It's looking in the daylight for a little blessing fish from God, and then throwing out your *amphiblēstron* to capture the moment and not forget it.

And to me, my *amphiblēstron* just looks like I have open eyes and a heart willing to see the positive things. When one blessing pops up, when one memorable event happens, I start looking around to see what God is up to and what else is on the way.

Looking at the last 24 hours of your life, what's a little gift God has given you? What's a small blessing, a small gift, a little fishy reminder that He is on your side and you should not give up?

Journal a prayer today, asking God to help you learn how to catch the lovely daily moments like Simon and Andrew caught fish.

1. "amphiblēstron," *Trench's New Testament Synonyms*. Available online at *studybible.info/trench/net*.
2. Argile A. Smith, Jr., "Fishermen in the First Century, *Biblical Illustrator* (Nashville, TN: LifeWay, Summer 2013), 8.
3. Ibid.
4. James A. Patch, "Fishing," International Standard Bible Encyclopedia, James Orr, ed. (Wm. B. Eerdmans Publishing Co., 1939). Available online at *internationalstandardbible.com*.

DAY 2
AGKISTRON

It was a simple fishing pole on which I caught the fish that hangs in my parents' living room. If memory serves me correctly, it was just a bright, plastic worm looped onto the end of a hook that brought the eight-pound beast down.

I was standing on the end of a rock when I caught him. It felt like the tug-of-war of a lifetime. But, spoiler alert, I won. And 25 years later, he still hangs in the living room, an homage to one of my prouder moments.

Just one fish. Just one pole. Just one huge victory for me that my parents still proudly (or not so proudly) display. One fish is all Peter needed, too.

READ MATTHEW 17:24-27.

What's the problem Jesus faced?

How did Jesus tell Peter to solve the problem?

By the way, you know Peter. He's also called Simon, and he's the same fisherman who was throwing out his *amphiblēstron* in yesterday's study.

Jesus told Peter to throw out his line, hook and catch one fish, and pull the money out of the fish's mouth. (That has never happened to me when fishing, by the way.)

The word Matthew chose here to talk about the method of fishing in Matthew 17 is only used once in the whole Bible—right here. It's a different kind of fishing—it's the focused, singular, purpose-driven fishing.

> *agkistron* (noun) — a fishing hook; a small hook[1]

This is the word for the kind of fishing I do. This is literally a line and a hook. In fact, this word means "hook."

This type of fishing, with just a line and a hook, has a singular purpose—to catch a fish. Catch *one* fish. And in Peter's case, catch *the* fish.

Every year for my birthday, I take about two hours to myself to think, pray, journal, and listen. I have a goal—to have one Scripture for the year, to listen to God and feel Him direct me toward the words that will shape my year.

It's like I go fishing. Just this year I went down to Leiper's Fork, Tennessee, and sat at a picnic table with my Bible and journal. I had a worship album playing through my headphones and I started to journal, thanking God for the last year and asking Him for direction this year. A passage of Scripture I heard at church on Sunday came to mind.

READ PHILIPPIANS 2:12-18.

Apparently I'm not allowed to complain this year, according to verse 14. (We'll see how that goes! Ha!) But as these verses came to mind, I felt like I was fishing for some direction from God and these words hooked onto the end of my rod.

How would my year be shaped if I built around the ideas in this section of Philippians? That's what I continued to journal about. For example, the passage said that if I were to "do everything without grumbling or arguing," I would shine in the world "like stars in the sky" (vv. 14-15). Talk about lovely! Not grumbling or arguing is a visible symptom of a bigger picture—it shows to the world that we're working out our salvation (v. 12), that we're holding firmly to the Bible and what it teaches (v. 16).

As a bonus, when we're not grumbling or arguing, we can be more singularly focused on looking for the loveliness that God is working around us.

How would those verses shape your year?

Like that fish in my parents' living room, I caught these verses and hung them up on the wall in my room. I wanted to see it, remember the experience, and let them shape my year. That's one example of what comes to mind when I picture looking for the lovely things in our every day with this particular method of "fishing." I think of the times when God has something specific for us—something specific for you—that will help you get through a hard time or help you know which direction you're meant to go.

It could be a verse, a prayer, a Facebook message, a text from a friend, or even a sunset. It may look like any of those things, but often for me, it feels like His love and provision. Just like Jesus allowed that fish to provide for Him and Peter, there are moments when it feels like God says something specific or shows me something unique. In those moments God reminds me how personally He loves me, sees me, and provides for me.

I'll never forget the first time I walked a new trail at Radnor Lake. My earbuds in, I walked on the dirt path for ten to fifteen minutes, thinking, praying, processing. Two particular situations were in my mind, one to do with an invitation I had received to speak at an event and the other to do with a single man in my life. Neither had a clear right or wrong answer to me—both were opportunities, options, chances that may be worth taking. I rolled them around in my head like marbles bouncing with each step I took.

I was worried, though. I was worried that I was going to miss what God had for me because I couldn't see the *right* or *wrong* of the situations. *Just show me, Lord,* I was saying, *and I'll do what You want. I just don't know where either of these are going.*

I was fishing. I was standing on the shore, pole in hand, asking God to provide what I needed for the situation.

I suddenly looked down and realized that I did not know where I was and I was pretty sure I was going the wrong way. Since I had never been on this trail before, I didn't know if I had possibly hopped onto the "difficult" trail or if I had somehow made a wrong turn. Everywhere I looked was brown path, green trees, and dark shadows. Frustration crept up my back and pushed on my shoulders as I realized I was feeling that same confusion in lots of areas of my life—particularly in those two situations that I couldn't get out of my brain while on this path. A little sure I was missing something, a little concerned that I was lost on the wrong path.

Then in a blink, God stamped a statement onto my heart: trust the path. If only I would trust the path that had been laid before me, I would get to where I needed to be.

> Your word is a lamp for my feet,
> a light on my path.
> PSALM 119:105

How does the Bible show us where to go?

"Trust the path," it seemed God was saying. And I knew He didn't just mean the new-to-me "medium" difficulty trail at Radnor Lake. God meant the questions in my heart, the things I wonder about, the worries that I'm going to miss Him. I don't have to know where things are going. I don't have to know the destination. I just have to trust God to be faithful on this path He's leading me down.

What's one way God has shown you His love lately?

How can you make time in your daily life to catch an encouraging moment? (Go on a walk, read your Bible, listen to worship music, etc.)

Do you make time now to connect with God on a daily basis? What does it look like when you do?

What does it look like for you to use your agkistron to be encouraged with just what you need at the right time?

Take some time today, even if it's just fifteen minutes, to sit and listen to God, read your Bible, connect with Him. Throw your line into the lake and wait, patiently trusting Jesus for the fish. The encouraging word you need, or the wisdom that makes all the difference, is about to be caught.

These passages may give you a jump start.

READ PSALM 37:3-7 AND MATTHEW 6:25-34.

What did God show you today? What's your catch of the day?

1. *"agkistron,"* Blue Letter Bible, Strong's G44. Available online at *blueletterbible.org.*

DAY 3
SAGÉNÉ

The sports I love, and the ones I've always played, are team sports. Soccer. Football. Synchronized swimming (with my sisters in our neighbor's pool). All things that teammates do together. I love being a teammate and watching teammates in action. Things seem to go better when many hands are involved, and when things go wrong, you don't have to stand alone in defeat.

My uncle helped me reel in that big fish that hangs in my parents' living room. I wasn't alone in it. We were a team with a fishing goal that day.

We've talked about two types of fishing nets already. Let's just peek at them again real quick. Match the word to the definition and the Scripture.

amphiblēstron   a hook   Matt. 17:24-27

agkistron   a casting net   Matt. 4:18-20

Today we're going to look at a net that needs a team. This is a story Jesus is telling—a parable—to help the listeners better understand the kingdom of God. This story is about judgment day, but what we're going to focus on is the actual net and the way the fishermen used it. This is a really interesting parable, worth your time to read and study. But for our purposes today, we're simply looking at the net type and how it was used.

> The kingdom of heaven is like a net that was let down into
> the lake and caught all kinds of fish. When it was full, the
> fishermen pulled it up on the shore. Then they sat down and
> collected the good fish in baskets, but threw the bad away.
> MATTHEW 13:47-48

Why did the fisherman have to sort through the fish?

Again, this is the only place in the New Testament where this word is used to describe for us another type of net.

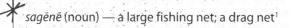

> *sagēnē* (noun) — a large fishing net; a drag net[1]

This net is also called a drag net. Most often used at night, this net requires multiple fishermen working together, usually in two parallel boats, to drop the huge net, around 16 feet in height and up to 800 feet long (Picture that! That's more than two football fields in length!). The fishermen let the weights (typically rocks) pull the bottom of the net to the sea floor. Then the *sagēnē* is pulled onto shore with ropes and all the fish around are scooped up.[2]

Once ashore, the fishermen must sift through the good and the bad fish, throwing back the bad, keeping the good.

Why does this net require multiple people?

My three best friends—Haley, Molly, and Misti—and I have a running group text message chain. We check in almost every day. Even though we don't all live in the same city right now, we're teammates. When we've read a good book we want to share, or when something hilarious has occurred, we talk about it. And when something is challenging, we all jump in together.

It's almost like we have our own version of Batman's Bat Signal. When someone says "I need y'all," we're there. We put our heads together, try to solve the problem, and try to find hope in the situation.

Do you have people like that? Who do you turn to when you need help?

I love the idea that our biggest catches, the most important things, require other people. I need my people—I need them to be there with me in the moment, and I need them helping me sort through and find the lovely in my every day.

I need my friends to do that for me, with me, around me.

What are the benefits listed of having people stand with you? Do you have a friend who comes to mind?

There was a man all alone;
he had neither son nor brother.
There was no end to his toil,
yet his eyes were not content with his wealth.
"For whom am I toiling," he asked,
"and why am I depriving myself of enjoyment?"
This too is meaningless—
a miserable business!
Two are better than one,
because they have a good return for their labor:
If either of them falls down,
one can help the other up.
But pity anyone who falls
and has no one to help them up.
Also, if two lie down together, they will keep warm.
But how can one keep warm alone?
Though one may be overpowered,
two can defend themselves.
A cord of three strands is not quickly broken.
ECCLESIASTES 4:8-12

My friend Heather and I went on a walk this week with her husband and two daughters. The leaves are changing and as we walked and talked, Heather just kept noticing the different shades of leaves. I was complaining about a situation that isn't changing as quickly as I'd like it to, and all the while Heather was noticing beauty in the change of seasons.

I needed that. I need my friends to remind me to look for the lovely moments in life, to collect them. Whether my day is going well or not, my friends help me to remember the way God has worked in the past and is working right now.

I love glimpses of friendship in the Bible. There's one in Job I want us to look at today. Job, as you may know, had some pretty terrible things happen to him. Really terrible things—his kids all died, his animals and servants were burned up, and he developed painful sores all over his body. There's nothing lovely about any of that.

READ JOB 2:11-13.

Later on, Job's friends weren't the best at helping him look for lovely, but I love this moment right here. Seeing them set out as soon as they heard, picturing them weep with him as soon as they saw him, and then to sit with him for seven days in the silence of sadness? That feels like really beautiful teamwork. Even in the silence, that feels like finding something lovely, doesn't it?

When I decided to move to Nashville, I sat on the floor at Haley's house and the girls and I cried. We just cried. We knew it would be sad to leave each other and for me to live in a different city. They didn't try to change my mind or fix the pain; we just sat together and cried.

Now that moment has become a really beautiful memory of mine, because they were with me in it. That's all the lovely I needed—my people with me in my pain. And knowing they were with me, that I wasn't alone, made it possible for me to keep going, to finish the plan I felt God had started in my heart.

I think of Paul and Silas in Acts 16. They were in the prison cell, in a really bad spot, but they had each other. They fished together that night, kept the true things about God in front of their eyes, and my guess is that when doubt or fear tried to creep in, they tossed it out like a nasty old fish.

Who are the people you call on to fish with you—who pick through the net, helping you toss out the bad and keep the good?

Maybe send a text or call them. Do something to thank them today for standing with you, sifting through the fish with you, holding onto the net.

Sidenote: Perhaps you're feeling lonely, like there's no one fishing with you. Pray today and ask God for friends—ask for just one friend to come along and help you carry this.

JOURNAL THE FIRST PART OF PSALM 68:6
—AND BELIEVE IT.

1. "*sagēnē*," Blue Letter Bible, Strong's 4522. Available online at *blueletterbible.org*.
2. Smith, "Fishermen in the First Century," 9.

DAY 4
TAKING CARE OF YOUR NETS

After this session, I'm more impressed with fishermen than ever before! I knew it was a challenging lifestyle, but I guess I had never considered all the various ways to catch fish—how much thinking had to go into every net decision and how each way to catch fish required a different type of patience.

Before we move ahead, let's review our three types of fishing methods.

As a former elementary school teacher, I like visuals and comparisons and knowing how to apply what I've learned to my real life. This week, I've been walking around my life wondering who my *sagēnē* friends are, where my next *amphiblēstron* moment is, and setting aside specific *agkistron* time.

Fill out the chart below using information from the first three days of this session's study.

TYPE OF NET	WHO WAS USING IT?	WHAT DOES THIS METHOD LOOK LIKE IN YOUR LIFE?
amphiblēstron		
agkistron		
sagēnē		

When I think of the three methods of fishing, I summarize them like this:

In my life, the *amphiblēstron* net are the moments when I need to look around, eyes wide open, and see what God is already doing around me. Then I need to grab onto those moments and remember them, cherish them, and be encouraged by them.

What's a situation in your life where you need to fish like that?

I've always wanted to be a mom, but I haven't had that chance yet. But something I've been doing recently is spending a lot of time with my friends' kids. I take them to the park or to get popsicles; I watch their baseball games and their choir performances. It feels like I'm getting to collect all these really beautiful moments with children, even while I hope and wait to have kids of my own one day.

For me, the *agkistron* method of fishing are my times alone with God. When I'm before Him, asking for Him to reveal Himself to me, through His Word, nature, or other people.

When has God revealed Himself to you recently?

My counselor mentioned how I have taught myself to temper my desires out of the fear of being disappointed. She really challenged me to open my heart again and let myself feel the longing and desires that God has put in my heart. So as I'm spending time in the Word, I'm reading all the verses I can find about longing and desire. Each time it feels like an opportunity to fish for some specific growth that God has for me in my personal life.

Sagēnē, as you have probably figured out, would be my favorite net. Even in the darkest nights, I love having other people around me, helping me collect the truths I need to hold tightly and people who just help me in my everyday life to accomplish the tasks before me.

When have you needed other people to be around you?

I wanted to hang twinkle lights in my office, but I couldn't do it alone. I called my friend April and she came to help. I wish you could've seen it—with no ladder, but a 15-foot ceiling, a desk, some stools, and some chairs, we managed to string lights across the ceiling. It did involve taping a baseball to the end of the strand and throwing it back and forth, but it worked! I needed April's help—not just to catch the baseball, but her being there reminded me I'm not alone. Looking up at those lights now reminds me of the loveliness of friends and teamwork.

Each net has grown to mean a lot to me, and I think about them each as I go through my day.

Another interesting thing kept popping up in my reading of biblical fishermen stories.

> Going on from there, he saw two other brothers, James son of Zebedee and his brother John. They were in a boat with their father Zebedee, preparing their nets. Jesus called them, and immediately they left the boat and their father and followed him.
> MATTHEW 4:21-22

What were John and James doing with their nets when Jesus found them?

> One day as Jesus was standing by the Lake of Gennesaret, the people were crowding around him and listening to the word of God. He saw at the water's edge two boats, left there by the fishermen, who were washing their nets. He got into one of the boats, the one belonging to Simon, and asked him to put out a little from shore. Then he sat down and taught the people from the boat. When he had finished speaking, he said to Simon, "Put out into deep water, and let down the nets for a catch." Simon answered, "Master, we've worked hard all night and haven't caught anything. But because you say so, I will let down the nets."
> LUKE 5:1-5

What were the fishermen doing with the nets when Jesus got in their boat?

There's some amount of upkeep and repair needed to the nets, isn't there? As John, James, and Simon all had to do with actual nets—washing, inspecting, and mending them to bring in their catch—we have to do with our proverbial nets and fishing rods that we've been discussing all session.

I've been rolling this around in my mind … what does it actually look like for us to "take care of our nets"? How can we set ourselves up for success when it comes to collecting moments like a fisherman collects fish?

I've brainstormed some options below. Fill in the blanks of your thoughts as well (and if you are studying with a group, definitely be ready to share your ideas!).

Type of Net	What does care look like for me?	What does care look like for you?
Amphiblēstron	Keeping a positive attitude, looking around for blessings, choosing to focus on God	
Agkistron	Having a journal with me, practicing listening to God	
Sagēnē	Being honest with my friends when things are hard, helping others look for the lovely, too	

Which type of fishing is most natural for you? The most difficult? Explain.

Finally, I think there are specific benefits to each of these that I want you to see. Just like real fishing, this is going to take some practice, perseverance, and choice. But it'll be so worth it. We'll look at one Scripture for each to see the benefit outlined for us.

Amphiblēstron

I remain confident of this:
I will see the goodness of the LORD
in the land of the living.
PSALM 27:13

How can you work to see the goodness of God every day? What benefits do you see as a result of putting in that work?

Agkistron

> Call to me and I will answer you and tell you great
> and unsearchable things you do not know.
> JEREMIAH 33:3

How does this verse explain the benefits of setting aside time to connect with God?

Sagēnē

> As iron sharpens iron,
> so one person sharpens another.
> PROVERBS 27:17

How does this verse explain the benefits of letting other people partner with you?

I don't know about you, but I officially now know significantly more about New Testament fishing than I ever thought I would! But I hope you're like me in that I'm excited about what it will look like to make these three things an active part of my life.

How does that start for you today?

WOMEN OF INFLUENCE

In 2015, the U.S. women's national soccer team won the World Cup. It may have just been a blip on your life's radar screen, or maybe you, like me, are a huge fan of soccer and so you watched every game and kept up with the storylines and cared so much that there may or may not have been tears at some point when the trophy was hoisted by the American team.

No?

Well, that's how I feel about soccer. And the fact that our women won the World Cup for the first time since 1999 was beyond amazing.

Our 2015 Women's World Cup Champion team is made up of 23 pretty amazing women. I'm not personally friends with any of them (yet), but because I'm a superfan, I know too much. I read the articles written about them, I follow stories through tournaments and season play, I watch the pieces that the sports stations make, and I look at the players' Instagram and Twitter accounts.

One thing that's the same for every team member? They all have lives outside of soccer. Soccer is their job and their passion, but they have families, non-profits, passions, pains, and struggles. Those things don't go away for the 90 minutes of the game, but while their worries and passions may run in the background of their mind, the game at hand has to be in the forefront.

Perhaps it's that way for a lot of us. We have issues, concerns, and worries that go on in our lives, but that doesn't mean we can leave homework unfinished or stay home from school until the pain is resolved. Being a woman of influence (and spoiler alert, you are) often means outwardly holding it together even when you may inwardly be struggling, hurting, persevering, or processing.

But how do we find the balance between honesty and faking it? How do we carry on even when our hearts are broken?

The women we'll look at this session chose to look at what God had placed in front of them, trusting that He would take care of their suffering and the concerns that burdened their hearts.

GROUP GUIDE

WELCOME!

Before you begin discussing this session's personal study, talk as a group about what you've found during this study as you've looked for lovely. What lovely things have crossed your path? If you haven't already, go ahead and read the session introduction on the previous page together as a group.

AS WE BEGIN, DISCUSS THE FOLLOWING QUESTIONS WITH YOUR GROUP:

Read Philippians 2:12-18. Do any of those verses stand out? Which ones? How would those verses shape your year?

What's one way God has shown you His love lately?

Who do you turn to when you need help? Brag on your best friends!

Which type of fishing discussed this session is most natural for you? Which is most difficult?

WATCH THE VIDEO:

To hear more from Annie, download the optional teen girls' video bundle to view Session 5 at *lifeway.com/girls*.

NOW, LET'S TALK:

How do your friends help you collect moments that matter? How do you remind each other about God's faithfulness?

What are some ways Jesus modeled friendship?

Who influences you? Whom do you influence?

PRAY:

Pray together as a group that you will learn what it means to be young women of influence this week. Thank God for all the ways He helps us to look for lovely in our lives.

DAY 1
MARY

I tend to overshare. It's been a lifelong problem (or gift?). I have a hard time deciding what should be private. In general, I think it is because I like for my friends to be informed about my life—that plus a love of storytelling equals *everybody knows too much.*

God has been tempering that in me. Not changing my personality or my desire to share with my people, but teaching me the beauty of keeping some things to myself. Whether it's little moments of God's faithfulness as I look for lovely, or me watching something new bloom, I feel Him encouraging me to hold some things close to my chest—to ponder them and keep them private.

There's strength there. I'm gonna show you.

> READ LUKE 2:1-20.

> *Who's the woman of influence in this story? What makes her deserving of that title?*

Many of us have heard this story over and over again, whether it's from reading the Scripture or hearing Linus recite it in *A Charlie Brown Christmas*. It's the birth of Jesus and the shepherds being told about it from the angels.

> *What did the angels tell the shepherds?*

> *What did the shepherds do once they found Mary, Joseph, and Jesus?*

> But Mary treasured up all these things and pondered them in her heart.
> LUKE 2:19

> *Circle the two things Mary did with what the shepherds told her.*

The Gospel of Luke tells us that twelve years later Mary had another experience like this.

READ LUKE 2:41-52.

What are "these things" that Mary treasured in her heart?

I can't imagine the pressure, concern, and emotional weight of being the mother of Jesus—and I'm not just talking about when He was doing His disappearing act in these verses, but all the time—from the first revelation and every day afterward. It seems that, at least twice, God gave Mary a peek into His heart and His plan for Jesus and, in many ways, His plan for her. And she just kept it to herself, treasuring up these lovely moments.

How do you think it helped Mary to hear these things about Jesus when He was an infant? What about when she heard about His experience in the synagogue as a preteen?

How does it help to have a heart that looks for lovely in a season of perseverance?

One of the most valuable things I've ever seen is the crown jewels of Scotland. From the outside of the old stone building, you'd never assume it's any different than the ten others that surround it on every side of the cobblestone square. You can tour all the buildings on this square within the walls of Edinburgh Castle. The rooms have been restored to how they looked hundreds of years ago, and they're filled with tourists daily. When I lived in Edinburgh, I made the trek into the castle grounds a few times, because I didn't want to waste the opportunity I had to live in a city *with a real castle*.

When a group of people from my home church were in Edinburgh, this was our first stop. After passing through the gates to the beautiful overlook that stares at all of Princes Street, we walked around the cannons and the old chapel and ended up at that cobblestone square. We entered the door on the left, where the crown jewels are guarded. My friends and I got in the line to enter the tiny, dark door and weave through some centuries-old hallways. Within a few minutes, we were suddenly staring at The Honours of Scotland, the crown jewels. They are tucked away, in the center of Edinburgh Castle, in a place you (or a thief) might never think to look. But it sure makes that building extra special. From the outside, it looks like every other building, but it's worth more than the others because of what it has inside.

How does that compare to what we know about Mary?

I see it in my life too. On my journey toward a healthier and stronger body, I've spent a lot of time in the last year focusing on my health. But it hasn't been a public venture, in fact, it's been extremely quiet. I exercise alone. I manage my food alone. I try on clothes alone. And every little victory is a winning moment for me and it has been between me and God. I treasure each one and having those valuable little moments inside makes me stronger, makes me look at myself differently, like I have a little victorious secret that no one else needs to know about. Now I'm sharing with you, though. Obviously, I am no longer keeping this just for me.

Here's what's interesting. Mary told, too. Obviously, right? Because if we look at this chapter (Luke 2), I imagine Mary must have sat down with Luke and told him many stories of Jesus' life since they're written down now. Do you think that's how he knew to write about the manger? I would guess it's how he knew to write about the things she treasured in her heart.

That's how we know about the crown jewels. Just because they were deep inside ordinary-looking walls doesn't mean they were less valuable. If we know where to look, we can all see them and share in appreciating their worth.

At some point, it's right to hold things in your heart, and at some point later, it's right to talk about them. To share the treasures that are in you. As you look for lovely and collect those moments, it's right and good to keep some of those treasures between you and God. At other times, it may be right and good to share them with others.

How does treasuring things in your heart make you stronger? How does it add beauty to your life?

Mary was a mighty woman of influence, and if you ask me, she was strengthened in these two important moments. When she rolled that information—about who Jesus was—around in her mind and hid it in her heart, it gave her power and strength when she reflected on that knowledge days and years later. She persevered through so much in her life—I wonder how often she recalled these two moments, these two treasures, and held onto them for hope.

What does that look like in your life?

There's one interesting thing that I can't get past. Look at these two verses again.

> But Mary treasured up all these things and pondered them in her heart.
> LUKE 2:19

> But his mother treasured all these things in her heart.
> LUKE 2:51B

"Pondered" is an interesting word, and the transliteration is used only six times in the Bible.

> *symballō* (verb) — to throw together, to bring together; to converse, to bring together in one's mind, confer with one's self, to come together or meet; to encounter in a hostile sense, to fight with one, to bring together of one's property, to contribute, aid, help[1]

So when the shepherds prophesied about Jesus, not only did Mary treasure it in her heart, but she kept going back to it, encountering those words over and over. But a few years later, Mary didn't have to tumble the words around. Just treasure them.

List some things you are treasuring in your heart. Then list victories or lovely moments that were treasured first and now you've had the opportunity to share them, like the crown jewels?

SECRET TREASURES   SHARED TREASURES

---

1. *"symballō,"* Blue Letter Bible, Strong's 4820. Available online at *blueletterbible.org.*

DAY 2
ESTHER

Have you ever read the Book of Esther before? It's like a television drama we would gather our friends around to watch for on a weekly basis. Even today as I was reading through it, I found myself amazed at some of the details and story pieces that I often forget.

If you've got about twenty minutes, read the Book of Esther. Yeah, the whole thing. Eleven chapters. I promise it's more entertaining than what's on cable right now. And in order to follow our path, it would be great for you to know the whole story.

We have lots of TV shows about what kind of lives are possible for women who seemingly have unlimited budgets: fancy parties, clothes for days, extravagant homes, and in some cases, surprisingly hard lives.

But before we go there, let's talk about how fancy King Xerxes' life was. (Answer: Wowie zowie fancy.) Also, just to note, many translations call him King Ahasuerus. Yeah, he's fancy enough to have two king names. So whether it's Xerxes or Ahasuerus, you're about to read about the lifestyles of the rich and famous.

READ ESTHER 1:1-9.

How long did King Xerxes "display" his wealth (v. 4)?

How would you describe the garden party that King Xerxes threw?

Yeah. Super fancy. I can't help but wish for a picture to go along with this description! Gold and silver sofas? I want to see it! In this little section of Scripture we get a pretty solid idea of what kind of luxury Esther was moving into.

Being a woman of influence, one who has power and position and favor, can have some real benefits, like golden couches. But it comes with responsibility, lack of privacy, unique problems, and unique opportunities.

Esther understood that. And whether you have influence in entertainment, at school, on the field, or in your home, you're a woman of influence. Your voice matters. How you handle yourself publicly matters. No matter how you got here, you're here and you matter.

READ ESTHER 2:1-8.

How did Esther come into King Xerxes' harem?

Was Mordecai in Susa by force or by choice? Was Esther in Susa by force or by choice?

Sometimes I forget that Esther was a prisoner in her own city. The part of the story we don't know is what it looked like the day she was picked up from her home in Susa and taken to the king's palace. Were some of her friends also brought to the harem? Did her neighbors cry when she was taken away? Was there a young man who caught her eye, whom she daydreamed about marrying and raising a family with, who watched his dreams be carried away to the king's future?

This matters to me because I think of Romans 5:3-5. Fill out the chart below from earlier in the study.

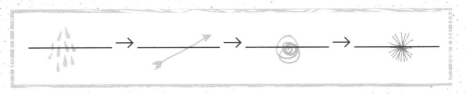

Even though we don't read about it, Esther certainly suffered here, maybe not physically but emotionally. You're a woman just like her, and you can imagine, like I can, what it would be like for your future to be taken from you, because some king you've never met needs a new queen who you don't want to be. Unique problems and unique opportunities.

READ ESTHER 2:9-18.

What did Esther gain because of her favor?

What would you imagine perseverance to look like during Esther's year of preparation to see the king?

I wish we knew Esther. I wish we knew her personality and her quirks and her emotions. That we see great strength in Esther once she became queen makes me think her perseverance paid off during that year of preparation.

If you've read the story before, or if you've spent time reading the Book of Esther today, then you know how dramatic the story becomes—Haman wanted to kill all the Jews, and Esther's uncle told her to ask the king to save the Jews at the risk of her own life, as going before the king without an invitation could lead to death.

Esther is portrayed as smart, capable, and pretty brilliant at orchestrating things correctly as she approaches the king to ask for his favor over her people.

But we can also tell that she was nervous and uncertain.

READ ESTHER 4.

What did Mordecai ask her to do?

What two reasons did Esther give for not wanting to go to the king?
1.
2.

What kind of insecurities do you think Esther might have felt considering the king hadn't requested her presence in 30 days?

What does it look like to move forward in your calling even when you feel insecure or nervous?

I had a pretty nasty breakup on a Sunday night before I had to go teach fourth grade on a Monday morning. I remember thinking, *My heart has to make it through today, do my job, do what I'm here to do, and then go home and fall apart.* There was a strength required in me that day—to stand up when I wanted to fall down.

Is there a time you had to show strength when you would've rather been weak? If so, explain.

Character produces hope.

Looking back at Esther's life, what made her strong enough to step into the role of influence over the king?

There's so much more to Esther's story, but what intrigued me is the courage that exuded from her in the moment, even though fear was present before. Something was built in her character, in her heart.

She had the power of the Queen, the influence of a royal, and clearly the strong heart of someone with influence. But don't ever forget, that she was taken from her home as a young woman and thrown into a situation that brought pain and insecurity. We can assume that Esther never forgot the life from which she was removed.

Esther was called upon to do something really difficult in a situation she didn't want to be in to start with.

Can you relate to that? When have you been somewhere you didn't want to be, but you could sense God working there?

Take a minute to think and process Esther's story. Part of the beauty of studying the Bible is that the Holy Spirit can bring back to you what you've learned, particularly in moments when you need it most. Record a prayer, thanking God for Esther's example of leading even through hard times and heartache. Ask the Holy Spirit to remind you of this lesson. And if you feel like you're in this kind of season right now, journal about that too! Tell God your hurts and worries and concerns. Ask Him to give you a persevering heart like Esther's.

DAY 3
LYDIA

I never set out to be a female entrepreneur. I always dreamed of being a schoolteacher, of having a classroom that was full of creative bulletin boards and tons of bookshelves bursting at the seams. I dreamed of a life where I graded papers at home on Sunday afternoons while watching the Atlanta Falcons play football and hurried to school Monday morning to warmly greet my students.

And I did that for five school years before the opportunity opened to pursue writing and speaking as a career. Suddenly, I wasn't working for someone else anymore; I was running my own company. Perhaps there's a club at school you joined as a freshman just because you thought it sounded fun (like yearbook). Now it's just a few years later and you suddenly find yourself president of that same club. You might ask yourself, *how did this happen?*

No training. No plans. No history of desiring to be a businesswoman. I'm just a girl who loves to write, and after years of hard work, it turned into a company: Downs Books Incorporated. That's us. Well, that's me. (And my part-time assistant.) Now, on a daily basis, I face decisions and problems and opportunities that I do not know how to manage or handle. It's scary and hard and sometimes I want to quit. To be fair, I actually have quit twice in my heart, but God always brings me back around after I whine and complain a bit.

There's one female entrepreneur in the Bible whom I totally love, even though we don't know tons about her: Lydia.

READ ACTS 16:11-15.

What do we learn about the city of Philippi, where Paul and Silas have stopped (v. 12)?

On what day does this story occur? Who is the first group that Paul and Silas speak to on this day?

(I love that. I love that in the busiest city in the region, these guys chose to sit down with a gaggle of gals.)

What do we learn about Lydia from verse 14?

Using this part of Scripture, check what we know (and don't know) about Lydia.

A statement about Lydia	We know this IS true.	We know this IS NOT true.	We don't know from the text.
Lydia lives in Philippi.			
Lydia deals in purple cloth.			
Lydia is observing the Sabbath.			
Lydia worships God.			
Lydia grew up in Thyatira.			
Lydia lives alone.			
Lydia rejected Paul's message of Christ.			
Lydia is married with kids.			
Lydia works alone.			

A statement about Lydia	We know this IS true.	We know this IS NOT true.	We don't know from the text.
Lydia has multiple employees.			
Lydia is a successful businesswoman.			
Lydia dreamed of running her own business.			
Lydia had hard days as a female entrepreneur, but she didn't quit.			

We know Lydia moved from her hometown to the big city, but there's so much we don't know about her, isn't there? I know, the chart was not that challenging to fill out, but I did that on purpose. I want you to see how much we don't know for sure. (Yes, many scholars assume she was successful because she was able to provide for people she invited into her home, but it's not explicitly stated in the text.) Yet I hope you said that you know it's true, even though, again, it isn't explicitly stated.

How do we know that's true?

I'll answer with you: We know that's true because we know what it's like to be a young woman, we know what it's like to want to quit, we know what it's like when something feels too hard. And you, like Lydia, and me, probably know what it's like to work at something that matters to you and hope to be successful.

What are some things, though not outlined in Scripture, that may have been worries and concerns for Lydia?

She's mentioned by name one other time. We've been here before, in Acts 16.

READ ACTS 16:16-39.

What happened after Paul and Silas were persuaded to hang out at Lydia's house?

Can you imagine? You've invited these dudes over and next thing you know, they've been arrested for setting a slave girl free. But look at the last verse.

> After Paul and Silas came out of the prison, they went to Lydia's house, where they met with the brothers and sisters and encouraged them. Then they left.
>
> ACTS 16:40

Where do Paul and Silas go once they are released from prison?

Who is there to meet with them?

So, according to this Scripture (again, written by Luke who told us that Mary treasured things in her heart), Lydia's house became the meeting place for the church of Philippi.

How cool is that? A small town gal turned businesswoman turned hostess turned church planter.

What are some responsibilities of someone who is hosting a church meeting at their house? What do you imagine Lydia did to prepare for those meetings?

I love that Paul and Silas found her hospitable, generous, and open-hearted. I love that even though Lydia was trying to run a company, she also ran a home and a small group. It feels like her influence is palpable, doesn't it? Lydia had concerns, worries, a household, and a company to manage!

Where do you think Lydia found beauty in her life?

Where do you think she found purpose?

One of my favorite parts of Lydia's story is that when we meet her in Acts 16:13, she's a successful businesswoman who's observing the Sabbath down by the river with her friends.

Last year, when I got to go to Israel, we celebrated a Sabbath, or Shabbat as they say, in Jerusalem. From Friday night at sundown until Saturday night at sundown, the city literally stops. No shops are open, no electronics are used—no phones, computers, dishwashers, nothing.

What I did see, over and over throughout the city as I walked the streets on that Saturday, were groups of friends standing around talking. No rushing from here to there, no head down looking at your phone as you walk. No hurry. At all.

Though, to be fair, I'm still wrestling through what it looks like for me to add Sabbath to my every week. If I disappear from the world one full day a week, I'll miss a lot of fun and connection with my friends, since Shabbat isn't something celebrated across my whole community.

Instead, I'm finding little moments to walk away. An hour with my phone off (Gasp! Yes, off.), a day hanging out with friends and putting an auto-responder on my email letting people know I'll be back tomorrow. Making a choice, like Lydia, and getting together with my pals to catch up. That's what she was doing. She was hanging out with her friends by the river on the Sabbath. Before Paul arrived, maybe they were talking about God or maybe they were talking about food and new recipes.

Whereas I can convince myself that a woman of influence has no time to take a day off or rest or put her phone down and walk away when there's work to be done, Lydia shows us that isn't true. And just to be clear, it wasn't that she didn't have fabric that needed to be dyed or laundry that needed to be done or family to care for. She allowed herself a break.

What Sabbath shows me is that in order to catch up to the demands of my life, I have to rest. When I choose rest on a regular basis, I actually accomplish more when I'm working. God's kingdom economy just works like that.

The slower I go, the more my eyes can focus on what's right in front of me. It's like the difference between standing in Times Square with all the billboards and bright lights and standing on the beach when the sun sets. I need Sabbath. I need to choose quiet and rest and slowness, even when I'm trying to run a business and home and small group and relationships, because the quiet shows me the lovely that's right in front of my eyes.

Sabbath helps me look for lovely in unique ways. And, as we see in Lydia's life, it was right in the middle of the Sabbath that God opened her heart (Acts 16:14) and changed her life. I think that's something to be remembered.

Do you already observe the Sabbath well in your life? If not, what would it look like if you did?

Over the next few days, try to find a day when you can relax with some friends (by a river or not, your choice) and observe Sabbath. How would you better see the lovely things in front of you if you chose to slow life for a bit—a day, an hour, an afternoon—and just breathe?

DAY 4
YOU

I'm not the mother of Jesus. I'm not a kidnapped teen-turned-queen trying to save her people. I'm not a female entrepreneur hosting the first house church in Philippi.

When I look at the lives of the women we've studied this session, I feel very different from them. Not just because I have Internet and air conditioning, but because my story is so unlike each of theirs. At the same time, I have so much in common with them. And you do, too. The same God. The same gender. The same ability to influence.

You matter. (So do I.) You're a woman of influence. (So am I.) You're impacting people around you every day—whether it's your classmates or your friends or your Instagram followers or the barista at your local coffee shop. You need Sabbath. (So do I.)

When I was reading through the Bible, so many women came to mind who were influential in the sphere God had given them. And it seemed, over and over again, that they each went through the Romans 5:3-5 process.

Again, what are the four steps?

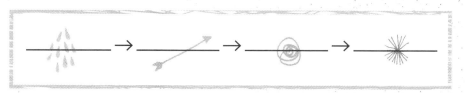

READ ALL OF 2 CORINTHIANS 4.

How can you fix your eyes on "what is unseen" in your current situation (v. 18)?

How did Mary fix her eyes on what was unseen? What about Esther?

NOW REREAD VERSES 17-18.

For our light and momentary troubles are achieving for us
an eternal glory that far outweighs them all. So we fix our
eyes not on what is seen, but on what is unseen, since what
is seen is temporary, but what is unseen is eternal.
2 CORINTHIANS 4:17-18

What verses stand out to you when you consider your places of influence?

I love verse 16: "Therefore we do not lose heart." That's another way of saying *we have hope*. We don't lose heart because we've seen that our sufferings cause us to choose to persevere, and when we do that, our character grows. And then, hope! So much hope.

Where are you influencing right now? In real life and online? Make a few notes of how you're influencing in these areas.

HOME

SCHOOL

CHURCH/FAITH

SOCIAL MEDIA

Underline the places where you feel like you're currently having to choose to rejoice in your sufferings. (Where is it hard right now?) Now put a heart beside the place where you're full of hope. And finally draw some arrows around where you're persevering through a difficult time.

I wish we could see Mary, Esther, and Lydia's answers to this as well. If you're studying along with a group, I hope you'll share openly about this part.

List one way you've found lovely this session in each area of life.

HOME

SCHOOL

CHURCH/FAITH

SOCIAL MEDIA

Share that as well, either with friends, those at your church, or take a picture and share online using the hashtag *#lookingforlovely!*

Session 6

JESUS

The day in July when I turned 33, we had a picnic. I wore a yellow dress and we had a dairy-free cake. My friends brought balloons and one of my buddies popped them at the end of the party and I pouted. We snacked and kids ran around the picnic tables as the sun set behind the Tennessee hills and fireflies slowly rose from the grass.

As I laid down that night, besides being thankful for my friends—a little embarrassed at my balloon-popping pity-party and really happy about that yellow dress—I thought about 33. That year, that number, had long stood out to me.

Now, here, I'm the same age as Jesus was when He died.

When I look around my life, at the men I hang out with who are also 33, I picture Jesus with the same amount of wrinkles, the same few gray hairs peeking around the edges. I picture Him sitting around a bonfire with us in my friend Matt's backyard. I picture Him as one of us. Because 33.

I'm 35 now. I've outlived Jesus' life on earth. And that's one of the strangest truths for me to process. I like to remember that He was human. I like to think about the humanness of Him, the part of Him that tasted Earth. His Godness is often discussed (as it should be)—He was perfect; He never sinned. But He knew Earth. He knew being fifteen; He knew being five. He knew being twenty-seven and still single. Right? Can I get an amen?

I can hardly write about Him because I feel like I can't communicate my facial expression about how deeply I like Jesus. I love Him in a way that's deeper than even I know, but I also like Him so so much. He's who I want to hang out with. He's who gets me. He's the One who knows all the things and says He wants to hang with me anyways. Not in spite of, but right through. And I cannot wait to see Him face-to-face and hear His laugh.

To finish our time together in this study, we have to look at this Man. He found lovely in His every day, the good ones and the hard ones. He lived Romans 5:3-5. We have to see Him for who He is—He is Jesus, who suffered, who persevered, whose character was in place and yet tested constantly, and He is our hope.

GROUP GUIDE

WELCOME!
Before you begin discussing this session's personal study, talk as a group about what you've found in this study as you've looked for lovely. What lovely things have crossed your path? If you haven't already, go ahead and read the session introduction on the previous page together as a group.

AS WE BEGIN, DISCUSS THE FOLLOWING QUESTIONS WITH YOUR GROUP:

How do you know when to share and when to keep something to yourself?

When have you been somewhere you didn't want to be, but where you could sense God working?

Read 2 Corinthians 4:18. How can you fix your eyes on "what is unseen"?

Share the ways you're influencing right now (p. 102). How have you found lovely in each of those areas?

WATCH THE VIDEO:
To hear more from Annie, download the optional teen girls' video bundle to view Session 6 at *lifeway.com/girls*.

NOW, LET'S TALK:
Read Psalm 46:10. How do you process what God is teaching you?

In what ways can you practice Sabbath this week?

Our last personal study session is about Jesus. How do you think He persevered and looked for lovely?

PRAY:
Pray together as a group, thanking God for moments of rest. Ask Him to help you become more like Christ as you learn about Him this session.

DAY 1
JESUS KNOWS SUFFERING

I bet you're doing this by heart at this point. I know I am. About every third conversation I have right now, I'm talking about Romans 5:3-5.

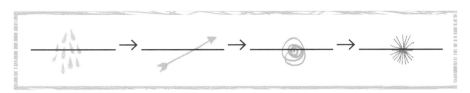

I'm talking about suffering. I'm telling my friends how hope isn't free. I'm sharing with them what I'm learning about how suffering matters more than I ever realized, how it's not something to be rushed through or something from which to beg God for rescue.

When we think of Jesus, we know He knew suffering.

READ ISAIAH 53:2-3.

How do these verses describe Jesus' relationship with suffering?

The King James Version of the Bible says Jesus was "a man of sorrows, and acquainted with grief" (v. 3). Doesn't that break your heart?

When we think of Him, obviously we think of how He suffered on the cross. You may have read this story before, but look at it with fresh eyes today. Jesus, a 33-year-old man, praying in the garden with His sleeping friends, begging God to come up with another way, but yielding His safety and protection for ours.

TAKE A FEW MINUTES AND READ LUKE 22:39-46,63-65; 23:26-46.

What stands out to you about Jesus' death, specifically when you think of His humanness?

It's just incredible what Jesus suffered in His body and, I'm sure, in His mind and spirit. I can't imagine it. What I've seen of it, thanks to movies like *The Passion of the Christ*, is practically unbearable to watch, and it's just an actor! It's not even the real guy, the One I love.

When I went to Israel, the only place that my emotions really took over was at the garden of Gethsemane. In my Bible, the verses that talk about Jesus in the garden in Matthew 26:36-56 are spread over two pages. I read those twenty verses over and over again as the tears puddled in my eyes. I stopped reading and just started to rub my hands over the words and talk to Jesus. It was here, I just kept thinking, in this very spot where His decision to sacrifice Himself for me, for all of us, was confirmed. His obedience brought our salvation. If I can't hug Him and thank Him face-to-face yet, I will rub the pages where His name and suffering sit, and pray my guts out in thankfulness.

The tears wouldn't stop. I kept telling myself to dry it up and calm down, but after two or three minutes, I gave into it. I decided to let my heart break. I knew that was the feeling of what was happening; it's happened a time or two in my life, but this was different. I felt His kindness. His kindness toward me in this place, in my sin, needing salvation. It broke my heart. I just let the tears fall as long as they needed to, knowing I may never stand in that spot again. My soul, my insides, my guts, they needed to say all the things that my mouth didn't know how to say. So I cried as I ran my fingers over the words of this story again and again, and I whispered, "Thank You. Thank You. Thank You." Because He suffered for me.

But it's not just in His death that He suffered. That's what I want you to look at today. The crucifixion, in all its bloody glory, is necessary to read, but Jesus' life was full of suffering.

JESUS SUFFERED WHEN HIS PEOPLE SUFFERED.

> [1] Now a man named Lazarus was sick. He was from Bethany, the village of Mary and her sister Martha. [2] (This Mary, whose brother Lazarus now lay sick, was the same one who poured perfume on the Lord and wiped his feet with her hair.) [3] So the sisters sent word to Jesus, "Lord, the one you love is sick."
> JOHN 11:1-3

How was Lazarus described in verse 3?

What happened to him in John 11:14?

READ JOHN 11:32-36.

Why was Jesus troubled? How did He respond?

Jesus loved His friends. And to see them suffer, even though He knew where the story was going (how Lazarus would be resurrected), brought Him pain. He wept. He hurt.

What has broken your heart like that?

JESUS SUFFERED WHEN HE WAS MISUNDERSTOOD.

> All the people in the synagogue were furious when they heard this. They got up, drove him out of the town, and took him to the brow of the hill on which the town was built, in order to throw him off the cliff. But he walked right through the crowd and went on his way.
> LUKE 4:28-30

Jesus was preaching in His hometown shortly after His ministry began. He read from a prophecy about the Son of God (vv. 18-19; see Isa. 61:1-2), and then made the (very true) claim that the prophecy was about Him. The crowd did not take this well.

How did the people there treat Him? How do you think Jesus felt?

Remember, just because Jesus was God and Jesus was perfect does not mean Jesus didn't have emotions. He did! And I would imagine it was heartbreaking and disappointing to watch people you've known your whole life get so unhappy with you that they try to throw you off a cliff!

JESUS SUFFERED WHEN HIS FRIENDS ABANDONED HIM.

Jesus knew, like you and I know, that friends aren't perfect. Humans are flawed. He knew He would be rejected and abandoned by His very best friends.

READ MATTHEW 26:31-35.

What did Jesus say to His friends? What was Peter's response?

READ MATTHEW 26:47-50,56.

Who led the crowd to Jesus? How was Judas described?

Why did all of this happen according to verse 56?

I'm a big fan of Peter. So I've read and taught on him often. He's the central character in what I think must've been one of Jesus' saddest moments.

READ LUKE 22:54-62.

What happened in verse 61? Who looked at Peter?

What does that tell you about where Jesus was compared to where Peter was when Peter denied even knowing Him?

I picture this scene in my mind. I see Jesus hear Peter's voice, turn just in time to hear him say that Jesus is just a stranger, not a best friend, and then they make eye contact. Ugh. It practically brings me to tears right now. What heartbreak for Jesus. Even though He is God and knew everything that was to come, His humanness here—His 100 percent feels-like-a-person—must've just crumbled with sadness. So He suffered. Over and over again. And this is just the tip of the iceberg.

What are some other stories from the Gospels that come to your mind that show how Jesus suffered in His life on earth?

Jesus suffered in death so that we wouldn't have to, but He suffered in life so that we would see it's survivable, and so we could see that strength comes from holding on.

Today, and all session, let's pray and thank Jesus for being Jesus; for His Godness and His humanness. And today particularly, journal a prayer thanking Jesus for the ways He suffered on our behalf.

DAY 2
JESUS CHOSE PERSEVERANCE

When I was a student the University of Georgia (go Dawgs!), our campus ministry did a 21-day fast every fall. Most people fasted a type of food or technology, but a few hardcore folks went all in and did the full water-only 21-day fast. (That was not me. Just to be clear. Give me smoothies or give me death.)

Unfortunately, at the same time of that season was the height of the intramural football tournament. The best team from UGA would face the best team from Georgia Tech at halftime during an Atlanta Falcons game at the Georgia Dome.

Our ministry's team was good, but more than half the team *wasn't eating for three weeks.* As the Dome got closer, and our team kept winning, I couldn't believe what I was seeing. These poor dudes who hadn't had any nourishment were moving closer and closer to playing during a professional football game. And sure enough, they did it. They won within the teams at UGA and then they played in the Dome ... on Day 19 of the fast. Incredible.

They persevered without appropriate nutrients in a way that I don't endorse or recommend or think would be possible for anyone outside of the 18 to 22 year-old window. They chose to compete, even when they weren't in their best shape, because they wanted to win the game. They wanted to come out on the other side of that Falcons game proving what we've long believed: UGA is better than Georgia Tech. (That's not a biblical truth, just an opinion. Proceed as such.) But their victory taught me something about perseverance and strength.

Just like Jesus modeled suffering for us, He also modeled perseverance for us and showed us how He gained strength from His ability to hold on.

READ LUKE 4:1-13.

Jesus was filled with the _____ _____ *AND led into the desert by the* _____ _____.

I don't love that. Is that OK to say? It's just hard for me to picture the Holy Spirit filling me and then walking me into something hard. It happens; it's just hard.

Do you feel like that has happened to you? When has the Holy Spirit blessed your life and then walked you into a desert season?

How did Jesus feel after fasting for 40 days (v. 2)?

Hungry? Just "hungry"? Yeah. I think that's an understatement.

In this story, Jesus was tempted by the Devil three times, and each time He persevered. Jesus persevered even when He was in need.

REREAD LUKE 4:3-4.

What did the Devil offer Jesus? What need did this reveal in Jesus?

How did Jesus respond to the Devil?

Jesus was showing us that persevering, even when our body is in need, benefits us. What Jesus needed was food. What you may need is healing, financial provision, or direction for yourself or someone in your family. The list of needs could be everlasting, couldn't it?

They are legitimate needs. I have friends who have cancer and are waiting to be healed. I have friends who are waiting for a baby to grow in their bellies. I have friends who are without a job and cannot make ends meet and so they wait.

But what Jesus shows us is that sometimes we're meant to persevere through our need, trusting that the provision God supplies is enough.

Where are you in need? What would it look like in your life to persevere like this?

For me, today, my need is physical. I have a disease (PCOS) that I want God to heal in my body. I do all the things doctors instruct, but I still need full healing because PCOS can make getting pregnant very difficult (and I hope to do that someday). So, what does it look like for me to trust that God provides and that His provision meets my needs even when I don't see it?

READ DEUTERONOMY 8:3 (THAT'S THE VERSE JESUS QUOTED TO THE DEVIL IN THIS SECTION).

"Man does not live on bread alone," but by what?

So when it comes to my healing, I turn to the Word and I believe what it says about God being a healer, and I wait. I wait believing that He is who He says He is, that His Word is true, and that His ways are higher than mine.

Sometimes this is exactly how we look for lovely. Our circumstances may be pretty grim—there probably wasn't anything beautiful about being hungry and alone in the desert—and it's hard to find lovely in our situation. Those are the moments when we can turn to God. He's always lovely, and His Word speaks to His loveliness in all 66 books.

JESUS WAS OFFERED COUNTERFEIT POWER IN THE PRESENT, BUT PERSEVERED FOR THE ETERNAL POWER IN THE FUTURE.

READ LUKE 4:5-9 AND THEN RESPOND TO THE FOLLOWING QUESTIONS.

What did the Devil offer Jesus? What need did this reveal in Jesus?

How did Jesus respond to the Devil?

I don't think this necessarily means that when an opportunity comes your way, you say no to it. But I do see times in my own life, and times in my friends' lives, when a shortcut appears that looks very enticing with all it offers, but it's clearly a shortcut out of the pain or waiting.

For Jesus? He knew in the long run that He would receive all the worship and all the power.

READ PHILIPPIANS 2:9-11.

Who will worship Jesus? How many knees will bow?

So Jesus knew what He was being offered would eventually be His anyways, and in a much greater measure. But what Satan was making available to Jesus was earthly power now, no more suffering, in exchange for Jesus' worship.

When have you been offered a counterfeit version of the real thing? Have you ever been tempted like that?

I see it in myself a lot when I think of sex before or outside of marriage. There's a healthy and beautiful victory after the waiting, but there are repeated counterfeit opportunities trying to tell me (and all of us) that the wait isn't worth it, that what would be offered now is better than what will be gifted later.

Again, Jesus gives the exact answer to help us know how to counteract such an offer.

Fear the LORD your God, serve him only and take your oaths in his name.
DEUTERONOMY 6:13

We worship God and serve Him only. We don't serve ourselves—serving our own best interests, serving what we can't resist, serving our own desires—we serve God. We serve His heart, His desires, and we worship Him alone.

How does serving and worshiping God alone help us look for lovely in the midst of waiting?

JESUS PERSEVERED EVEN WHEN HIS FAITH WAS QUESTIONED.

READ LUKE 4:10-12.

What did the Devil offer Jesus? What need did this reveal in Jesus?

How did Jesus respond to the Devil?

Satan went for the jugular at the end. He asked Jesus if He *really* believed that God was God and that God would actually take care of Him.

When have you questioned that God was going to take care of you?

It's crossed my mind a lot. When things go differently than I think they will, when a relationship doesn't work out, when my heart is hurt or my body is injured or my people are hurt, I can hear that same whisper: "Didn't the Bible say God loves you, Annie?" I hear the snake's tiny voice in my ear, "And is that what you feel right now?"

Jesus' answer to the Enemy of our hearts? *Don't test God.* I love this because Jesus didn't feel the need to defend God at all. He didn't even give a nod to Satan's suggestion. Why? Because Jesus knows God's heart.

Match the truth with the Scripture.

You are loved.	1 Peter 2:9
You are chosen.	Zephaniah 3:17
You are cared for.	Jeremiah 31:3
You are delighted in.	Nahum 1:7

That's just four examples.

What's your favorite verse that reminds you of God's heart for you? Journal it here.

We test someone or something when we need to know its worth our ability. We are tested in order to be able to drive and we are tested in classes to see what we know.

Jesus didn't have to test God. Because He already knew. So He persevered in what He knew. He found lovely, because He knew exactly where to look—at His Father.

DAY 3
JESUS SHOWS CHARACTER

It's an interesting thing to picture Jesus' character growing. Wasn't He God? Doesn't He know all the things? Was He an emotional grownup in a kid's body? I don't think so. I think He grew and aged, like every other kid does. Jesus was perfect in all His ways, but His maturity grew.

I can't be sure of this, but just like Jesus had to learn to speak and how to walk, I think the same was probably true of His emotions and character. Luke 2:52 tells us "Jesus grew in wisdom and stature, and in favor with God and man." Jesus learned and grew as He aged.

I love this story about Jesus pursuing maturity and growth.

READ LUKE 2:41-52. (WE READ THIS LAST SESSION, BUT LET'S LOOK AT IT AGAIN FROM A DIFFERENT ANGLE.)

How old was Jesus in this story? How often did the family make this journey?

So, Jesus was familiar with the temple and the Feast of Passover. They probably parked the camels in the same place every year, near the same families and friends, and had the same traditions. Thursdays are for the big fish fry and stuff like that. I've grown up going to the same camp every summer since I was ten. I've missed about five summers in my life. I know the place pretty well and the longer I'm there, the more comfortable I become. I imagine that was something like Jesus' experience in Jerusalem.

Why did the rest of the family leave Jesus behind?

How many days did it take them to find Jesus?

Where did they find Him? Whom was He sitting amongst when they found Him?

I totally get Mary's response. Don't you? What stands out to you about what she said?

Pay attention to the definition of *character:*

> *character* (noun) — the mental or moral qualities distinctive to an individual[1]

Based on what you know, and what we've studied so far, what are some words you would use to describe Jesus' character?

Circle the words you think describe Jesus' character.

kind	strong	anxious	dedicated	compassionate
fun	proud	servant	bitter	trustworthy
angry	easily	frustrated	humble	weak
patient	focused	mean	forgiving	sarcastic

Two stories showing Jesus' character displayed strongly stand out to me.

READ MARK 6:1-6.

How did the crowd respond to Jesus in verse 3? How is He described here?

What are some other ways Jesus could've reacted when the people He grew up with and had known His whole life turned against Him?

How would you respond in a similar situation?

The Internet is a funny place, right? I mean, a day rarely goes by that someone in the faith community doesn't get trolled, discouraged, or gossiped about. For all the reasons I love Twitter, that's one of the reasons I don't. Watching strangers, and sometimes friends, say terrible things about other believers is really hard for me, whether I agree with them or not.

It happens off-line too. Whether it's someone questioning our motives when we genuinely thought they were pure, or an old friend giving a polite but not supportive nod to our recent ministry venture.

How did His time in the desert prepare Him for this interaction?

How do you think God used *this* moment in Jesus' life to prepare Him for the future, when His friends would abandon Him?

READ JOHN 13:1-17.

When did this story happen?

What had Jesus previously done at Passover (think of the story when He was 12)?

Right. This was a very memorable time in Jesus' life. He also knew something unique about this particular year, His 33rd year on the planet.

What did He know (v. 1)?

What did Jesus do for His disciples that night? What was Peter's response?

(Clearly I love how Peter responded. That guy is the best—*all or nothing*, y'all. *All or nothing.*)

What's the big deal about washing feet? (Think about what you know about the shoes they wore, the condition of the roads, Jesus' role in the group, etc.) How does this show Jesus' character?

Think back to when the Devil tempted Jesus in the desert. Which of the three temptations lines up well with what Jesus did here?

Though the Enemy offered Jesus power, Jesus chose instead to serve. The strength of His character came from His perseverance through suffering.

Line up Romans 5:3-5 again.

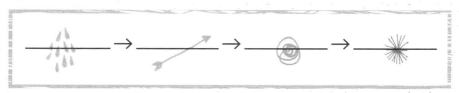

Think for a minute and journal about how you see this path in Jesus' story and life.

How can your character improve to be more like Jesus?

1. character, *Oxford Dictionaries*, 2016. Available online at *http://www.oxforddictionaries.com/us/definition/ american_english/character.*

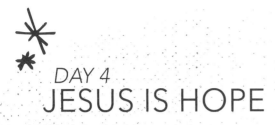

DAY 4
JESUS IS HOPE

This is where we say goodbye, and according to me, there's no better way to end. This journey together, looking for lovely around the different curves, through different professions and people in the Bible, to here. To Jesus, our Hope.

How have your thoughts on hope changed so far in this study?

We know hope comes at a cost. Thinking about that, how does Jesus embody hope?

Paul, an apostle of Christ Jesus by the command of
God our Savior and of Christ Jesus our hope, ...
1 TIMOTHY 1:1

What does it mean to say Jesus is "our hope"?

Why would Paul start his letter like this?

I think Peter may have given us the secret key to how Jesus is our hope.

Praise be to the God and Father of our Lord Jesus Christ! In
his great mercy he has given us new birth into a living hope
through the resurrection of Jesus Christ from the dead.
1 PETER 1:3

What kind of hope do we receive through Jesus' resurrection?

Jesus is our living hope.

GO WITH ME HERE. FLIP TO ROMANS 5 AGAIN.

Jesus displayed suffering, perseverance, character growth, and hope. He *is* our hope. So clearly, as described in Romans 5:3-4, there's a hope that we have to process through to have.

But then Peter calls it a living hope.

So what if after we have suffered, persevered, and allowed our character to grow, Jesus infuses life into the hope that has been deposited in our hearts?

I'm picturing a row of dominoes that you've earned one at a time, and then, once you have them all, you use your finger, or maybe blow on it like a candle, and they begin to move and fall and look like they have life of their own.

What's the difference between hope and living hope?

And hope does not put us to shame, because God's
love has been poured out into our hearts through
the Holy Spirit, who has been given to us.
ROMANS 5:5

What's true about hope? Why doesn't it disappoint?

So this living hope must come from a living source, right? Ahhh. The resurrection of Jesus. He's alive, and so is the hope He offers to us.

READ FROM HEBREWS THROUGH THE EYES OF LIVING HOPE:

We have this hope as an anchor for the soul, firm and secure.
It enters the inner sanctuary behind the curtain, ...
HEBREWS 6:19

How is Jesus an anchor for your soul?

It has been an interesting journey for me lately, processing through these steps to get to where I have more and more hope—looking for lovely, learning to rejoice in the hard things, choosing to persevere when I want to quit, and allowing my character to be built. But then, when it comes time to hope, I'm scared.

I'm realizing that I have to trust the process, trust that as God is walking me through Romans 5:3-5 that includes choosing to hope. That hope isn't centered on my abilities or myself at all. When I'm scared to hope, I remember that my anchor isn't me— it's Jesus. Jesus is the anchor of my soul. So when I feel like hoping for something could make me float away into an ocean of fear or disappointment, I remember that Jesus holds me, protects me, and keeps me calm. He is my hope.

This, friend, is why we cannot quit. This is why we have to keep looking for lovely. Because in the end, your soul is anchored to a living God. That hope, it anchors you. It holds you steady.

What words describe the anchor in Hebrews 6:19?

We've seen Jesus embrace every element of this. Using the chart that follows, fill out thoughts or verses or ways you've seen Jesus display each one. Then, if you're brave enough, journal a short prayer in each box, asking God to increase each area in your life. I did it too, because I need it.

	SUFFERING	PERSEVERANCE	CHARACTER	HOPE
JESUS				
ME	God, help me not to wimp out of suffering when it feels too hard.	I want to be the kind of woman who perseveres, God. Show me what that looks like for me.	Deepen my character. Make me more like Jesus.	Fill me with hope, God, and the living kind! Let me always be covered in it.
YOU				

I'm at Think Coffee Shop in New York City. I'm sitting at a high top table and thinking and praying about what we do with this living hope. I want to understand it for me and for you. My Bible—it's one of those big heavy versions, not the digital type—just crashed to the ground in epic style, and as I picked it up, I saw this verse. And I realized it's exactly where I want us to end.

> May the God of hope fill you with all joy and peace as you trust in him,
> so that you may overflow with hope by the power of the Holy Spirit.
> **ROMANS 15:13**

Friend. That's my prayer for you. May the God of hope fill you with joy and peace, even as you're suffering, persevering, and allowing your character to grow, as you look for lovely and trust in Him. I pray you do trust in Him, more than ever before—trust in His timing, trust in His plan and His seasons—so that you may overflow with hope. I pray that your life will be marked by hope because you do not give up. I pray that you've found lovely and you continue to collect moments that matter.

Amen and amen. You're a finisher, and I'm proud to know you.

Session 7

NOW WHAT

In early March, I sat with a friend and we were talking about New Year's resolutions. Sort of in passing, she said, "but obviously, everyone has quit their resolutions by now."

I smiled. "I haven't," I said.

I took a new perspective on New Year's resolutions this year. I did a New Year's experiment. I changed my view. How would my life be different if I stuck to this idea, this experiment, for just one year? Now I look toward the finish line as a place where the hope rests, where my character has been built, and where I see the fruits that are harvested through seasons of waiting. It hasn't been easy; I've wanted to quit, but in those pressure-filled moments, when quitting would be the easiest way out, I think of you. And Jesus. And farmers. And fishermen. And musicians. And the woman of influence I want to be.

So, now what? That's the question, isn't it? Now that we have finished the study (fist pump to you for getting to the end!), what happens now?

Now everything changes. If you don't believe me, try it. Try to be the one of your friends who doesn't give up. Try to be the one who looks for and sees the lovely. You'll notice, really quickly, that your life isn't the same. You aren't the same young woman you used to be. Your outlook on trials—while still painful and unpleasant (and we should be honest about that)—has shifted to a realization that you are starting Romans 5:3, and you are willing to do the hard work of those verses to get to the hope in Romans 5:5.

Take Romans 5:3-5 and weave these verses into your heart. Make them part of who you are. Don't live a day without the truth of them. In every situation, find the spot where you are in this process and name it. You may be in multiple stages at the same time because of multiple opportunities, pains, or life circumstances. Look for the lovely in those places. Whatever you do, don't give up.

Then, hope. We rejoice in our sufferings—great and small—because they are giving us opportunities to grow in perseverance. That daily grind of perseverance is so worth it because without us even knowing it, the muscles of our character are growing stronger. During this study we have looked for lovely, found Jesus, and we have found hope. And that's a life worth living.

Annie

GROUP GUIDE

Before you begin discussing this session's personal study, talk as a group about what you've found this week as you looked for lovely. What lovely things have crossed your path? If you haven't already, go ahead and read the closing note from Annie on the previous page together as a group.

AS WE BEGIN, DISCUSS THE FOLLOWING QUESTIONS WITH YOUR GROUP:

What stands out to you about the story of Jesus' death, when you think of His humanness?

How does serving and worshiping God alone help us look for lovely in the midst of waiting?

What's your favorite verse that reminds you of God's heart for you?

How have your thoughts on hope changed during this study?

WATCH THE VIDEO:

To hear more from Annie, download the optional teen girls' video bundle to view Session 7 at *lifeway.com/girls.*

NOW, LET'S TALK:

What is the importance of collecting moments that matter?

What's your greatest takeaway from this study?

How can you continue to look for lovely and collect moments of God's faithfulness in your everyday life?

PRAY:

Give thanks for your time together. Thank God for bringing women and other girls into your life to study His Word with and to look for lovely together. Ask Him to help you continue growing more like Jesus every day. Thank Him for hope that anchors the soul.